ALL-TERRAIN
PUSHCHAIR WALKS
Snowdonia

Zoë Sayer and Rebecca Terry

Published by Sigma Leisure – an imprint of
Sigma Press, 5 Alton Road, Wilmslow, Cheshire SK9 5DY, England.

British Library Cataloguing in Publication Data
A CIP record for this book is available from the British Library.

ISBN: 1-85058-834-1

Typesetting and Design by: Sigma Press, Wilmslow, Cheshire.

Cover photograph: Snowdon Horseshoe from Snowdon Viewpoint on the A498 *(Copyright, Phillip Elsdon)*

Maps and graphics: Zoë Sayer and Rebecca Terry

Photographs: Phillip Elsdon, Zoë Sayer, Keith Jackson and Rebecca Terry

Printed by: Bell and Bain Ltd, Glasgow

Disclaimer: the information in this book is given in good faith and is believed to be correct at the time of publication. No responsibility is accepted by either the author or publisher for errors or omissions, or for any loss or injury howsoever caused. Only you can judge your own fitness, competence and experience. Do not rely solely on sketch maps for navigation; we strongly recommend the use of appropriate Ordnance Survey (or equivalent) maps.

Preface

The spectacular scenery of the Snowdonia National Park makes it a wonderful location in which to introduce your children to walking. It is great to get them out and about from as early an age as possible so that they can experience the delights of the world around them. There are many things to do while out walking, such as picnics, paddling in streams and animal-spotting. Every experience you give them increases their knowledge and understanding of our environment as well as increasing their capacity for and enjoyment of learning.

A pushchair is often seen as a hindrance; it's easy enough to push around town but how do you negotiate the obstacles found in the countryside? The advent of all-terrain pushchairs means that there is now no reason why having a baby should hinder our enjoyment of walking. In fact, 'access for all' is one of the main objectives of the national parks today. However, stiles and rocky terrain can be a problem and it is impossible to see such obstacles on a map. We have selected thirty pushchair-friendly walks in the Snowdonia National Park. All routes have been thoroughly tried and tested with babies in pushchairs, so you can now go for a walk with full knowledge of the route ahead.

The walks range from simple riverside rambles to full-on alpine-style stomps, so there is something for everyone. The simple 'at a glance' symbol key and grading system make walk selection easy. You can begin each walk knowing whether there are refreshments and changing facilities available allowing you to plan ahead. Each walk is also accompanied with suggestions of other ways to amuse the little ones in the area.

We have had great fun putting these walks together and hope that you and your children enjoy them as much as we did.

Acknowledgements

Special thanks to Rhodri and Jamie for being the test subjects for this book! Thanks also to Keef and Phil for accompanying us on many of these walks.

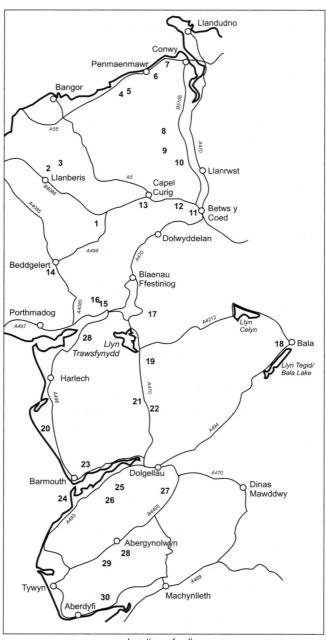

Locations of walks

Contents

Introduction

This book contains thirty walks in Snowdonia suitable for an all-terrain pushchair. There are both circular and "there-and-back" routes, and many can be shortened or have worthwhile detours. Walks range from 1 to 6 miles in length and cover a wide range of difficulty.

Snowdonia

Though Snowdonia conjures up images of pushchair-unfriendly, mountainous country, hidden amongst the peaks are a variety of terrains to provide varied walks to suit all tastes. The walks encompass the whole of the National Park, and range from gentle riverside strolls to isolated mountain valleys and even a beach – so we hope we have included something for everyone.

The walks are not exhaustive and are intended as an introduction to the area – there are many other suitable routes to explore once you know what is possible with a pushchair.

Routes and Grades

We have deliberately made this book as easy to follow as possible. Each walk is accompanied by a simple route map; this shows the start point and numbers referring to instructions in the text, as well as obvious features. The maps are intended to be used in conjunction with the relevant Ordnance Survey Explorer map, and the information on them is by no means comprehensive. Details of the relevant map and the starting grid reference are given in the walk summary.

Each walk contains an "at-a-glance" key which tells you all you need to know to prepare for the walk – distance, difficulty, any stiles, facilities such as toilets or ice cream vans and any hidden costs, so there shouldn't be any nasty surprises when you set off. You can also see whether the walk requires two people to overcome obstacles or if it can be accomplished solo.

The walks have a basic summary detailing points of interest and useful information on the area. We have also included an "in the area" section, suggesting nearby alternative activities for yourself and your family.

You should always allow more time than that recommended. Times given are approximate and based on a speed of two miles an hour. However, not everyone walks at the same speed and the times given do not make allowances for picnics, tantrum breaks or walking toddlers.

It should be noted that circular routes are written in the direction requiring the least effort and are not always reversible! If you are thinking of reversing a walk, read the description carefully to check it is possible.

Fitness

It is assumed that walkers will have a basic level of fitness. Those who consider themselves unfit should only attempt the easiest level of walk and, if necessary, take advice from their doctor. The hardest level of walk should only be attempted by those experienced in both mountain walking and all-terrain pushchair technique.

All-Terrain Pushchairs – Advice for First-Time Buyers

There are now many makes of all-terrain pushchairs (ATPs) on the market. For help in choosing an ATP, here are some of the factors we have come across in researching this and other books!

Ensure your child is old enough for the ATP. Many makes have a reclining position suitable for use from birth, but bear in mind that very young babies should not be bumped around. Seek the manufacturer's advice and choose your walks carefully. Small babies (less than four months) should only be taken on the easiest level of walks and if you are not happy with the terrain, turn round!

Make sure the ATP has pneumatic tyres and good suspension to provide cushioning.

Lightweight prams are better! The walks in this book, however, have been carried out with a 14kg pushchair, but were much easier with a 7kg one.

Choose a long wheelbase, which makes leverage over obstacles

Single and Double All-Terrain Pushchairs from the 'Mountain Buggy' range. *Reproduced by permission of Chariots All Terrain Pushchairs www.pushchairs.co.uk*

easier than a short wheel-base. The front wheel should be fixed, or, at the very least, lockable. Rear wheels should be quick release.

Check that the push-chair folds easily and that it fits in the boot of your car!

Shop around, as it is always worth looking in the shops first and then checking the internet for the same pram at a better price – either new or used.

Accessories

A rain cover is essential, especially when out walking in the hills as the weather can change very quickly. Good quality footmuffs are easily available, if not already included in the price; fleece-lining and/or windproofing provides extra comfort.

Sunshades supple-ment the hood, which generally doesn't extend enough for walking uphill into full sun. Mesh shades are easier to walk with than para-sols.

A puncture repair kit and pump are strongly advisable for those emergency situations. You can also fill the tyres with a "goo" designed as an emergency fix for bicycle tyres, which prevents serious deflation.

We've found a pram leash useful, especially on walks with steep drops or steep descents. This is a strap, climbing sling or piece of rope tied to the pram handle and fastened to the wrist. This provides extra security should you accidentally let go of the pushchair, and is more secure than a handbrake.

What to take

For the baby:

* Pram with rain cover, sun cover, footmuff and puncture repair kit.

* Milk – if you are not breastfeeding, formula milk is easily carried in ready made cartons or powder sachets, then just add to water in bottles when you need it. If your baby likes warm milk, either carry warm water in a flask or make up extra hot milk and wrap in foil or a muslin.

* Nappies, wipes and nappy bag.

* Picnic – sandwiches are easy if your baby eats on his/her own, otherwise take fruit pots, yoghurt or anything easy to open. Don't forget a spoon and take all rubbish home with you.

* Snacks to cheer up a bored or peckish baby until you find a picnic spot. We have found that raisins or baby crisps keep them occupied for the longest!

* Water/juice

* Spare clothes. Layers are best as they can easily be put on or taken off as conditions change. Don't forget that though you may be hot walking uphill, your baby is sat still in the pushchair. Keep checking he/she is not too cold. An all in one fleece is a good buy. Look for one with fold-over ends to keep hands and feet warm – easier than gloves.

* Hat, either a sun hat or woolly hat depending on the weather conditions.

✳ Shoes for when your little one wants to get out.

For you

✳ Appropriate shoes (check the guide at the start of the walk) and coat. Keep a light waterproof in the pram ready for emergencies.

✳ Food and drink: it's very easy to forget your own in the rush to pack your baby's feast!

✳ Mobile phone.

✳ Small first aid kit.

✳ This guidebook and the relevant Ordnance Survey map for the walk.

The Countryside Code

✳ Respect – Protect – Enjoy

✳ Do not drop litter. Use a bin or take it home.

✳ Do not stray from public footpaths or bridleways.

✳ Do not pick any plants.

✳ Make no unnecessary noise.

✳ Keep dogs on a lead near livestock and under close control at all other times.

✳ Leave gates as you find them.

✳ Use gates or stiles to cross fences, hedges or walls.

✳ Do not touch livestock, crops or farm machinery.

✳ Keep the natural water supply clean.

✳ Walk in single file and on the right-hand side of roads.

✳ Do not cross railway lines except by bridges.

✳ Guard against the risk of fire.

✳ For information on new access rights, visit www.countysideaccess.gov.uk or phone 0845 100 3298.

Why walk?

✳ Walking makes you feel good

✳ Walking reduces stress

✳ Walking helps you see more of your surroundings

✳ Walking helps you return to your pre-pregnancy figure and ...

✳ Walking helps your baby learn about his/her surroundings and nature

Glossary of Welsh words

Here are the rough translations of some of the words you'll come across on the walks. This is not a comprehensive list, but hopefully some understanding will enhance your enjoyment of the area. N.B. Welsh words mutate – the first letter changes. In brackets are some common mutations you might see.

Aber	River mouth
Aderyn	Bird
Afon	River
Bach, Bychan	Small
Bae	Bay
Bedd	Grave, digging
Betws	Chapel, house of prayer
Brenin	King
Bryn	Hill
Bwlch	Pass
Cadair (Gadair)	Seat
Cae	Field, enclosure
Caer	Fort, citadel
Canol	Centre, middle
Capel	Chapel
Carnedd (Garnedd)	Cairn, rocky hilltop
Carreg	Stone, rock
Castell	Castle
Cefn	Back, ridge
Clogwyn	Cliff
Coch (Goch)	Red
Coed	Wood, forest
Craig	Crag, rock
Crib	Ridge

Croes (Groes)	Cross
Cwm	Valley
Cymru	Wales
Derwen	Oak
Dinas	Fort
Du (Ddu)	Black
Dŵr	Water
Dyffryn	Valley
Dynion	Gents
Eglwys	Church
Eryri	Snowdonia
Fferm	Farm
Ffordd	Road
Ffridd	Upland pasture
Ffynnon	Spring, well
Gallt (Allt)	Slope
Glan	Shore, bank
Glas	Blue, green
Gwyn, Wen	White
Gwynt	Wind
Hafod	Summer dwelling
Hen	Old
Hendre	Winter dwelling
Hir	Long
Isaf	Lower
Llwybr Cyhoeddus	Public footpath
Llyn	Lake
Llynnau	Lakes
Llys	Court
Lôn	Lane
Maen	Stone
Maes	Field, meadow
Mawr (Fawr)	Big
Merched	Ladies
Melin (Felin)	Mill
Moel (Foel)	Bare hilltop
Môr	Sea
Morfa	Sea-marsh
Mynydd	Mountain
Nant	Brook
Newydd	New
Oer	Cold
Ogof	Cave
Pant	Hollow
Pen	Head

Penrhyn	Peninsula, promontory
Pentref	Village
Plas	Mansion
Pont (Bont)	Bridge
Porth	Port
Preifat	Private
Pwll	Pool
Rhaeadr	Waterfall
Rhyd	Ford
Sarn	Causeway, pavement
Tal	End
Tan	Beneath
Toiledau/Cyfleustreau	Toilets
Traeth	Beach
Tref (Dref)	Town
Twr	Tower
Twysog	Prince
T ŷ	House
Tyddyn	Farmstead, small-holding
Uchaf	Upper
Ynys	Island
Yr Wyddfa	Snowdon

Some of the unfamiliar letter pronunciations for English speakers are as follows:

dd – *th* as in *the*

f – *v* as in *vole*

ff – *f* as in *ford*

th – *th* as in *thin*

rh – a breathy *r*

ll – put your tongue on your teeth and say "*lllll*" – a very soft "cl"

ch – back of the throat and breathe out, similar to the Scottish ch in loch

s – always soft as in *soft*

u – *i* as in *big*

w – *oo* as in *soon*

y – at the start of a word *u* as in *butter*

y – elsewhere, *i* as in *big*

e – as in *bed*

o – as in *top*

a – as in *dad*

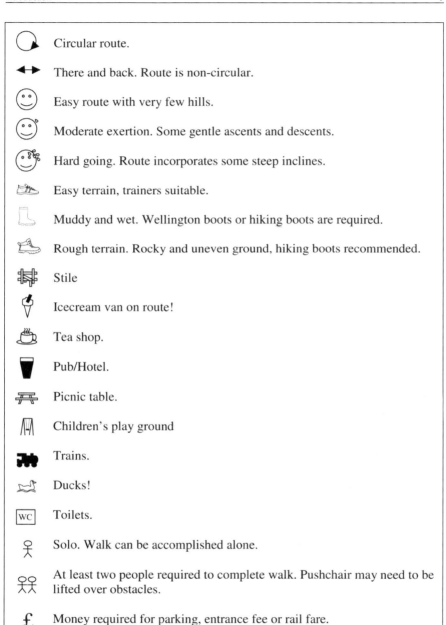

Circular route.

There and back. Route is non-circular.

Easy route with very few hills.

Moderate exertion. Some gentle ascents and descents.

Hard going. Route incorporates some steep inclines.

Easy terrain, trainers suitable.

Muddy and wet. Wellington boots or hiking boots are required.

Rough terrain. Rocky and uneven ground, hiking boots recommended.

Stile

Icecream van on route!

Tea shop.

Pub/Hotel.

Picnic table.

Children's play ground

Trains.

Ducks!

Toilets.

Solo. Walk can be accomplished alone.

At least two people required to complete walk. Pushchair may need to be lifted over obstacles.

Money required for parking, entrance fee or rail fare.

Key to symbols

Walk 1: The Miners' Track, Snowdon

Allow: 2 hours 30 minutes

I bet you never thought you'd get up Snowdon with a pushchair! Well, you won't get right to the top, but this walk takes you into the heart of the Snowdon horseshoe, with fabulous views, as far as Llyn Llydaw. There's also a tough extension up to Glaslyn for the adventurous.

The main walk is on an easy uphill track. This is the path miners used to take on their way to work in the Brittania Mine and was used to transport the ore, hence the name.

Map: Ordnance Survey 1:25000 Explorer OL17 – grid reference 648556

Distance: 3 miles (5km)

Getting there: Park at Pen-y-Pass car park (charge before 6.00pm).

Take the broad track through a wooden gate directly opposite the main car park entrance. Follow the track uphill.

To your left, you can see Carnedd Moel Siabod and straight ahead of you is Gallt-y-Wenallt. The track levels off and turns right.

In the valley below you, is a pipeline, leading to a hydroelectric plant far below. This pipeline was used in the James Bond film "The World is Not Enough" to represent a Kazakhstan oil pipeline!

1. Continue along the track past the small Llyn Teryn to your left.

   If it's clear you will now be able to see Snowdon (Yr Wyddfa) straight ahead of you, with the twin peaks of Y Lliwedd to its left. If it's not clear, Snowdon is the one with the most cloud on!

2. Where the track branches (by a small building) take the right branch along the edge of Llyn Llydaw towards a causeway. Just

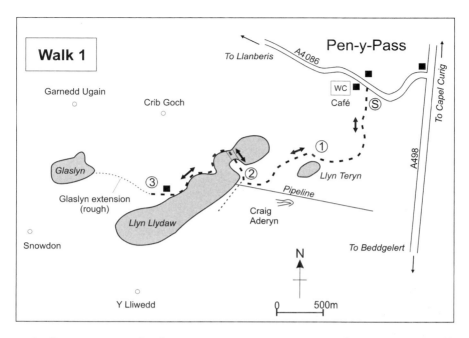

before you reach the causeway, you can get down to a small gravel beach on the shores of Llyn Llydaw, which is a lovely place from which to absorb your surroundings.

The causeway was built to carry copper ore down from the Brittania Mine.

Cross the causeway and head left along the opposite shore.

Up to your right are the crags of Crib Goch, an exciting knife-edge ridge. You might also see the smoke from the Snowdon Railway, as the train puffs its way to the summit.

Continue along the lake shore until you reach a ruined building.

This is the remains of the Brittania mill which worked the copper ore brought down from Brittania Mine. Brittania was the main copper mine on Snowdon and was transporting copper ore to Swansea and elsewhere by 1804, and in 1854 the mine employed over 180 men. The initial route for the ore was down the Snowdon

Llyn Llydaw from the Miners' Track

Ranger Path, but the route to Pen-y-Pass proved easier and what is now known as the Miners' Track was in existence by 1813. Ore was transported from the mill along this track, initially by packhorses and by 1907 this track was good enough for cars. The mine itself is further up by Glaslyn, and was originally linked to the mill by an aerial ropeway. The mine was worked, with intermittent stoppages until 1916, when production ceased for the last time.

3. A little further beyond the mill, the track becomes very rough and it is advisable to turn around here. The more determined can persevere up to Glaslyn (you will need to carry the pushchair over sections), where you will pass the main mine workings and gain a spectacular view down to Llyn Llydaw.

    Retrace your steps back down the track to the car park.

In the area:

The Snowdon Railway (www.snowdonrailway.co.uk): you can get to the top! The Snowdon Railway is a rack-and-pinion railway running from Llanberis to the summit of Snowdon (Yr Wyddfa). The railway has run since 1896 and spectacular views can be seen from the top on a clear day.

Piggery Pottery (www.piggerypottery.com) off the A4086 offers a fun day out for all the family. You can paint your own pot or pebble, have a go on a potter's wheel and take away your creation or watch experienced potters at work. There are refreshments and a children's play area.

Walk 2: Llyn Padarn, Llanberis

Allow: *2 hours 30 minutes*

Padarn Country Park is situated on the border of the old Dinorwig Slate Quarry complex that used to provide employment for 3000 men. In its heyday, roofing slates from Dinorwig were exported all over the world. When the quarry closed the site was purchased by the local council who regenerated the area into park land. The lake itself is the sixth deepest in Wales and is a site of special scientific interest due to the presence of an ancient fish, the Arctic Char. The lake is surrounded by beautiful woodland and there are fantastic views over the surrounding mountains.

The walk takes you on a circular route around the lake, with plenty of opportunities to stop and take in the spectacular views. This walk can also be done as an easy 'there and back' route for those who want to opt out of the difficult sections.

Map: Ordnance Survey 1:25000 Explorer OL17 – grid reference 559622

Distance: 5 miles (8 km)

Getting there: Turn off A4547 at Bryn Refail. Park in lay-by next to old stone bridge.

Walk down the road with the lake to your left. Go through the gate immediately in front of you (this gate is usually open but if closed you will have to lift the pushchair over), then follow the track ahead.

> As you walk around the first bend you are rewarded with great views across the lake, Llyn Padarn, and up the valley to the Llanberis Pass with Snowdon on the right. The entire walk is easy to follow as it is marked with wooden posts with a white band around the top.

1. Lift the pushchair over the next stile, turn right and walk along

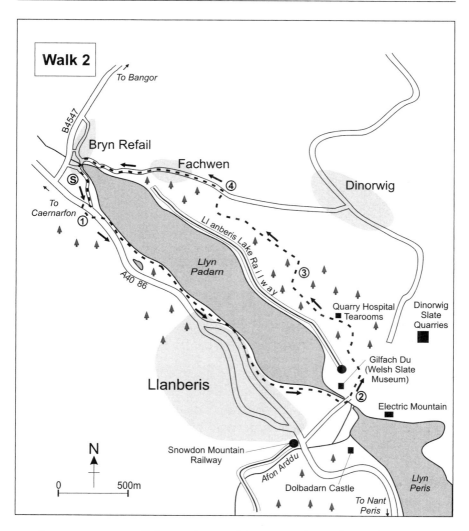

the grass verge of the main road (A4086) for a short distance. On the other side of the road you will see a wooden fence and a path. Cross the road carefully and turn left down this path. Follow the path down and through an old railway tunnel.

This tunnel and the track ahead are part of the old Llanberis to Caernarfon Railway. There are wooden benches along this dismantled railway track if you want to stop for a break.

As you continue along the track you will pass a pond on your right which is covered in water lilies in summer. After a further 5 minutes go through another barrier.

There are toilets on the right here but they are locked out of season.

Follow the lane ahead which takes you back to the main road (A4086). Turn left and walk along the cycle/footpath on the left-hand side of the road. This track brings you to a car park. Turn left immediately before the car park on to the path which runs alongside the lake.

There are picnic tables and a children's playground to the right of this path.

After a few minutes pass through a gate, cross over some wooden boarding and follow the path markers through a grassy meadow. You will soon come to a very narrow kissing gate. Lift the pushchair over the gate and continue to follow the path. At the end of the meadow turn left and cross the bridge between the two lakes.

The entrance to the Welsh Slate Museum, originally the workshops for the quarry, is now on your left. Entry to the museum is free. There are also craft shops, refreshments, the Lake Railway and toilets within the museum grounds.

2. You now have a choice:

If you want to do the easy 'there and back' walk then why not have a look round the museum before returning along the lakeside path the way you came.

If you fancy a challenge then the round trip is for you, so follow the directions below. The path is very rocky in places and there is a difficult stile to lift the pushchair over. However, if you are prepared to overcome these obstacles you will find it is well worth the effort. This route would be slippery and unsuitable for pushchairs in wet weather.

Take the road uphill directly ahead of you, not the road on your

Llyn Padarn and Llanberis

left to the museum. At the top of the road pass the front of the Quarry Hospital and Tearooms where you will be able to see the route markers again.

The path now goes up through an area of woodland and the tree roots and rocks under foot can make the going a little bumpy. You will soon come to a series of rock steps heading downhill. This is the most difficult section and it may be easier to lift the pushchair in places.

3. As you head downhill go past a sign on your left to the ruins of a wool mill and then you will see a kissing gate ahead. This is the last difficult obstacle. Lift the pushchair over the gate, turn right, cross over the stream and follow the track up the hill.

4. Follow the track for 15-20 minutes, ignoring paths to the left or right, until you come to the road. Turn left and walk along the road for 20 minutes until you reach the end of the lake.

Be careful! This is a quiet country lane but there may be an occasional car.

Turn left and cross the stone bridge and then left again onto the road where you left your car.

In the area:

Llyn Padarn Railway (www.lake-railway.co.uk) starts at Gilfach Ddu Station at the Slate Museum. The 60-minute ride takes you past Dolbadarn Castle and into Llanberis, as well as along the shore of Llyn Padarn. There are several stations at which you can take a break for a picnic and there is a café at the main station.

Greenwood Forest Park (www.greenwoodforestpark.co.uk) is a great day out with plenty to do for the whole family. There is a toddlers' village, little green run slide and a great sand play area. They can also meet bunnies, drive mini tractors and much more!

Walk 3: Dinorwig Quarries, Llanberis

Allow: *1 hour 30 minutes*

The Dinorwig Quarries were established in 1787 by Lord Assheton Smith, a major landowner in the area, and at one time were the second largest in the world (the largest being Penrhyn on the other side of the hill, which is still working today). In 1880s and 1890s, the quarry employed some 2757 men and had an output of 100,000 tons of slate each year, almost a quarter of the total Welsh slate output. Work was disrupted by a number of famous strikes over pay and conditions, in both Penrhyn and Dinorwig Quarries. The quarries were finally closed in 1969.

This is an easy walk which takes you round the old quarry workings. Though some see the quarry workings as a scar on the landscape, the sheer scale of the venture and the amount of rock which has been moved, mostly carried out without much hi-tech machinery, is impressive in itself. You are also rewarded with spectacular views up the Llanberis Pass, across to Snowdon and neighbouring hills, and down to the coast and Anglesey.

Map: Ordnance Survey 1:25000 Explorer OL17 – grid reference 590611

Distance: 1½ miles (3km)

Getting there: From the A4244, take the turning to Deiniolen at the top of a hill. Go through the village, and continue along the road. Head towards the slate heaps and park in the large lay-by just before a 'No Through Road' sign.

From the lay-by, follow the footpath sign to the left and through a small gate. Follow the path through young trees, until it opens out by some old quarry buildings.

> The long building on your left is dated 1925 and was a slate mill, for cutting and preparing the slates. The smaller building is dated 1921.

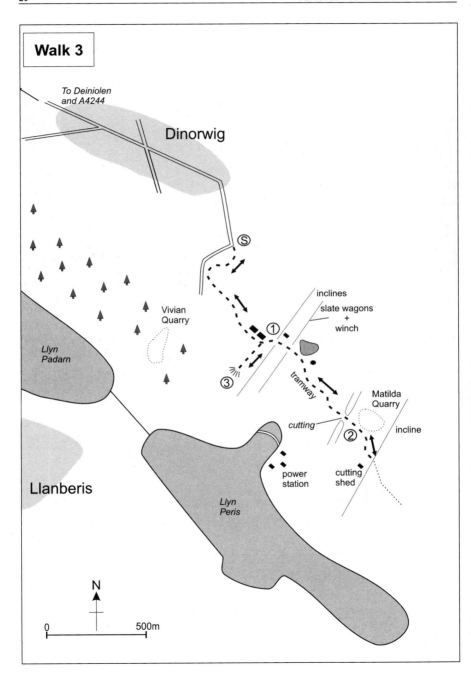

Walk 3

To Deiniolen and A4244

Dinorwig

Vivian Quarry

Llyn Padarn

Llanberis

inclines

slate wagons + winch

Ⓢ

①

③

tramway

Matilda Quarry

incline

cutting

②

power station

cutting shed

Llyn Peris

N

0   500m

Dinorwig Quarry, Llyn Peris and the Llanberis Pass

1. Go past the buildings and lift the pushchair over a large metal gate. Walk through the left-hand kissing gate. From here you start to get an idea of the scale of the quarrying. Follow the path round to the left.

Several inclines can be seen ahead of you, with a rusty slate wagon visible on the second incline from the left. As you walk along you will be able to see the remains of the winch system used to haul the slate wagons up the inclines.

The quarry developed in a series of terraces linked vertically by inclines to carry the slates, the first of which was built in 1789. From the 1830s, each terrace had a tram system - you are walking along one of the old tramways. Early slate transport from the quarry was by boat down Llyn Padarn (sunken slate boats have been found in the lake!) and then by cart to the coast at Felinheli (Port Dinorwig). Subsequently the Dinorwig Tramway (you drove along this to the car park) and finally the Padarn Railway was built and the railway ran until 1961.

Follow the path round to the right and downhill. You can see mining addits in the hill ahead of you and as you go into the dip, Llyn Peris can be seen in the valley below.

Llyn Peris is now the lower reservoir for the pump storage station. If the water is low, it has been pumped to the top reservoir and is being stored above your head! If the lake is full, the water has run through turbines below your feet to generate electricity.

Continue up hill, past the humming vent shaft for the pump storage station, and head towards the rock cutting.

Look for different colours in the slate. Dinorwic and Penrhyn slate is purplish-grey and is the oldest of the Welsh Slates (Cambrian, over 500 million years old). There are also green layers, due to chemical changes, and some of the purple slates have green spots and bands. The spots used to be circular, and give you some idea of how much the rock has been squashed in order to turn into slate.

2. Go through the cutting and have a look at the deep quarry pit on your left. Carry on along the track. Railway sleepers can be seen embedded in the path; evidence of the old slate tramway. Continue to the next cutting and head downhill until you see the remains of a large slate works and another cutting shed.

   Ahead of you is the Llanberis Pass and Snowdon. You can see Llyn Peris, Dolbadarn Castle and the entrance to Electric Mountain below you.

   Retrace your steps back to the kissing gate.

3. Go through the gate (lift the pushchair over) and turn left to the viewpoint with views of Llanberis and Moel Eilio opposite, Llyn Padarn and Anglesey to your right.

   Go back to the main path, past the quarry buildings and return to the car park.

In the area:

The Welsh Slate Museum (www.nmgw.ac.uk) is free for all and tells the history of slate industry in Wales and in particular the Dinorwig Quarries. There are slate splitting and forging demonstrations, a 3D film show, a giant waterwheel and shop. The café has highchairs and baby changing facilities and there is also a children's play area.

Electric Mountain (www.fhc.co.uk) has exhibitions and tours round the hydroelectric power station beneath the quarries. This power station has the largest man-made cavern in the world and was famously featured on Blue Peter!

Walk 4: Aber Falls, Abergwyngregyn

Allow: 1 hour 30 minutes

Aber Falls is one of the highest waterfalls in North Wales at 40m (130ft). The Welsh name is Rhaeadr Fawr, meaning "big waterfall". On a fine day, there are stunning views of the Carneddau mountains, though the falls are best after heavy rain!

The waterfall is reached by walking up a pleasant wooded valley alongside the River Aber. The valley is rich in history and biodiversity, with leisure and conservation side by side. Information on the past life of the valley is presented in an exhibition half way up the walk. There are plenty of picnic and paddling opportunities along the route.

Map: Ordnance Survey 1:25000 Explorer OL17 – grid reference 662720

Distance: 2¾ miles (4.5km)

Getting there: Turn off A55 at Abergwyngregyn. Drive through the village, following the signs to "Rhaeadr Aber Falls". Drive up a narrow country lane until you come to a car park and bridge. A second car park can be found over the bridge and first right. Both car parks are Pay and Display.

From the first car park: Cross over the bridge and turn immediately right along a metalled road. Turn right off the road down a gravel track and through a wide kissing gate.

From the second car park: Walk back down the road and turn left down the gravel track and through a wide kissing gate.

1. Head uphill from the kissing gate until you see an information board, which gives an outline of conservation work and ecology in the valley.

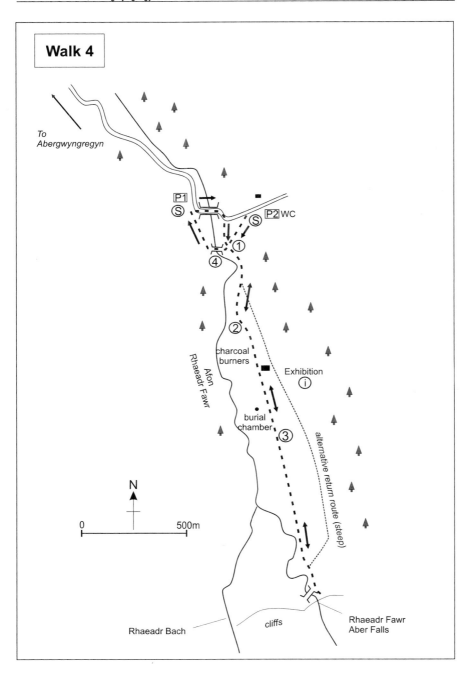

Walk 4

To
Abergwyngregyn

P1
S

P2 WC
S

①
④

②

charcoal
burners

Afon
Rhaeadr Fawr

Exhibition
ⓘ

burial
chamber
③

alternative return route (steep)

N

0   500m

Rhaeadr Bach   cliffs   Rhaeadr Fawr
Aber Falls

Go through the gate (there is a wide kissing gate if the main gate is locked) and continue uphill along the gravel track.

You will see the jagged hilltop of Bera Mawr straight ahead of you.

2. Ignore a path to the left through the plantation and carry on up the gravel track to a small exhibition building on the left, with picnic tables and benches.

Charcoal burners can be seen to the right of the path and many of the trees in the woodland have been coppiced for charcoal making – they can be recognised by numerous spindly trunks emerging from base of the tree. The exhibition gives a summary of life and industry in the valley through the ages.

Continue up the track with the plantation on your left and views of the Carneddau mountains ahead and to the right. Benches are located at intervals along the track.

Look out for the bronze age burial mound on your right. You may also see wild horses along the track.

3. The path narrows after the burial mound. Bear right along the track avoiding the steps. The track broadens again and continues to the base of the waterfall. As you approach the waterfall, there are several places where you can get down to the river side, though you will have to park the pushchair by the track.

The River Aber is the steepest river in Wales and England, though not on the section you've just walked! Over the falls there is a total descent of 70m, with the last 40m ending in a sheer drop. The waterfall is caused by a change in rock type, with the valley rocks eroding much more easily than the granitic rocks forming the cliffs.

A bridge and steps lead to the far side of the river, which is well worth a look for the view of the falls, but you will have to abandon the pushchair or be prepared for a steep carry!

Retrace your steps back towards the car park as far as the information sign. Here you can either head back along the road to the car parks or take the scenic route along the river bank.

4. 100m after the sign, turn left before the kissing gate you came through earlier. Go through a gate and over a wooden bridge to walk along the opposite river bank. Bear steeply right along a narrow path, which is rocky in places.

On the way to Aber Falls

Go down 21 easy steps, past a picnic table to a sculpture/bench. Head left past the sculpture to avoid steps up from the lower path. Go through the kissing gate (just navigable!) and back to car park 1. To return to car park 2, cross over the road bridge and turn immediately right.

N.B. It is possible to return from the falls through the plantation, but there are 3 ladder stiles (gates are locked). From the falls, follow the plantation sign. Lift the pushchair over the ladder stile and head up the steep, rocky path that cuts across the hillside. You may need to carry over small sections, but this is the worst part of the walk. On reaching the plantation, lift over the second stile and head down the path through the plantation. Ignore the sign to the historic feature as the path is not suitable for pushchairs. Lift over the third stile at the far end of the plantation and carry on down to rejoin the main track.

In the area:

Menai Straits Cruises (www.starida.co.uk) offer boat trips around Puffin Island off Anglesey and past the islands and bridges of the Menai Straits. Both trips offer views of spectacular scenery. Trips depart from and can be booked in Beaumaris.

Penrhyn Castle, near Bangor, (www.nationaltrust.org.uk) is a 19th-century castle built by the Pennant family, who owned the slate quarries at Bethesda. The castle is Victorian "nouveau-riche", with elaborate stonework and décor, and stands in 45 acres of gardens. There is a tea room, train museum, doll museum and art gallery.

Walk 5: Llyn Anafon, Abergwyngregyn

Allow: 3 hours

Llyn Anafon is a reservoir located up a quiet, picturesque valley west of Aber Falls. The valley is off the beaten tourist track and you can expect a quiet walk surrounded by the mountainous ridges of the Carneddau.

The walk is up a good track, initially along a coastal hillside before following a tumbling river in the valley floor. You pass archaeological remains and wild horses are common on the surrounding hills. Though the full walk is a long way, you can turn round at any point, and this beautiful valley is well worth a visit.

Map: Ordnance Survey 1:25000 Explorer OL17 – grid reference 676716

Distance: 5½ miles (9km)

Getting there: From Abergwyngregyn, follow the signs to "Rhaeadr Aber Falls". At the car park, turn left over the bridge and carry on up the hill for about 1 mile. Park in the small car park at the end of the road.

Go through the gate and follow the gravel track heading diagonally left up the hillside.

There are good views back down the valley to Anglesey.

Continue under the power lines and stop to admire the view to Puffin Island and the hills above Llanfairfechan.

On the hillside to your right is a large round enclosure. The round walls are Iron Age; the square walls are a modern sheepfold.

1. Before you pass under the wires a second time on this main track, take the grassy track forking off to the right. Carry on along this track, under the power lines.

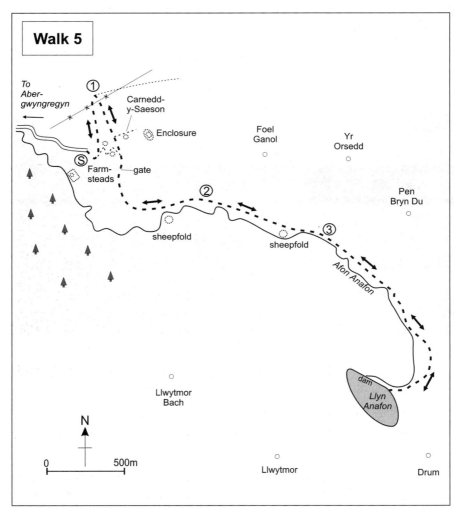

After about 200m is a round cairn to the left of the track. This is Carnedd y Saeson, a bronze age burial cairn.

Continue along the track to the gate, ignoring the zigzag track down to the right.

Below you on the hillside are two more round Iron Age farmsteads, one either side of the zigzag track.

Tha Anafon Valley

Go around to the right of the gate (slightly awkward) and continue up the track.

In the valley below you are the remains of a square enclosure (possibly Iron Age) – a farmstead with a square yard and the outline of a round house.

As you pass around the bend, you get your first view up the valley, with sheepfolds down to your right on the other side of the river.

2. Descend the track to the valley floor to walk alongside the river with plenty of grass for picnics!

The path starts to rise and is steep and rocky for about 50m before levelling off again.

In autumn, look for the contrasting yellow gorse and purple heather.

Carry on up the track, past white water rapids in the river.

To your right is the rocky top of Llwytmor and straight ahead is the rounded hilltop of Drum.

3. Continue as the track steadily rises and bends round to the right, following the river. Looking carefully ahead, the horizontal surface of the dam soon comes into view. Follow the track to the dam and Llyn Anafon.

The lake is in a cwm surrounded by the high peaks of Drum, Foel Fras and Llwytmor.

Retrace your route along the track to the gate. After the gate you can take a short-cut down the zigzag track to the left back to the car park.

In the area:

The Welsh Mountain Zoo (www.welshmountainzoo.org) is set in a large wooded estate above Colwyn Bay and has animals from all over the world. Once you've seen the animals, visit one of the cafés, have a picnic, play in the Tarzan Trail Adventure Playground or even play some great educational computer games.

Great Orme Mines, Llandudno (01492 870447), is the only Bronze Age copper mine in the world to be open to the public. You can visit the mine workings, walk along 3,500-year-old passages and see how our ancestors turned rock into metal. There is a visitor centre with gift shop and café.

Walk 6: Jubilee Path and Druids' Circle, Penmaenmawr

Allow: 3 hours

This walk takes you on the hills up above the North Wales coast, with spectacular views over the Irish Sea to Anglesey, Llandudno, Blackpool, and even the Lake District and Isle of Man on a clear day.

The walk starts off round the Victorian Jubilee Path, and then heads off across moorland on tracks to visit Neolithic stone circles. The walk can easily be split into two shorter walks, each of about 1½ hours' duration.

Map: Ordnance Survey 1:25000 Explorer OL17 – grid reference 730760

Distance: 4½ miles (6.5km)

Getting there: From the centre of Penmaenmawr take the turning to Sychnant. Take the third road on the right, just past a large chapel, Graiglwyd Road. Turn left up Mountain Lane, signposted to Green Gorge and Druids' Circle. Follow the narrow lane uphill until you come to two stone pillars. Park in front of the stone pillars.

Jubilee Path: Walk through the stone pillars, which mark the start of the Jubilee path. This is a level path round the front of Foel Lus.

> You can see Anglesey and Puffin Island to your left, and as you round the bend Great Orme comes into view. On a clear day you can also see Rhyl, Blackpool and even the Lake District and the Isle of Man!

There are steep drops to your left as you walk along the front of the mountain. As Great Orme, Conwy Mountain and the Sychnant pass come into view, the path narrows.

1. Continue until you reach a telegraph pole and a wooden bench

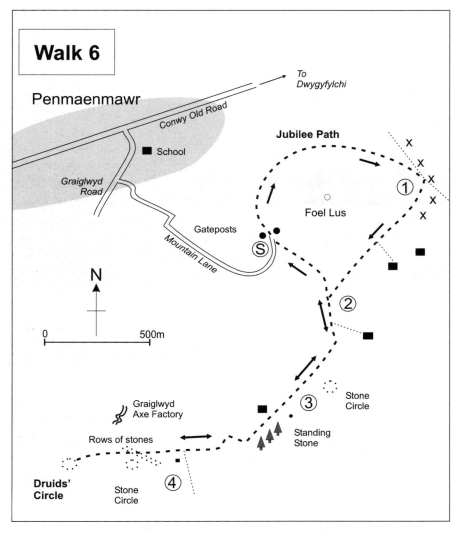

on your right. Turn right uphill to follow the line of telegraph poles. This is a narrow rocky path and awkward, so you may be happier pulling or carrying up this section.

The path levels off and broadens after about 50m and the going is much easier. Follow the path towards a wall and two houses, as it broadens out into a grassy track.

The Druids' Circle

2. When you reach a stony track, turn right to follow the wall. Ignore the next left turn and continue straight on (slightly uphill) until you reach a junction with a broad track. To return to the car park, turn right down the track.

   Druids' Circle: To continue to the Druids' Circle, turn left towards a No Entry sign and take the right-hand track. (To reach this from the car park, simply walk along the track with the stone pillars behind you.)

   Go through a metal gate and continue along the track beside a stone wall.

   If you look through a gate into the field to your left, you can see a couple of stones sticking up which form part of a small stone circle, one of many ancient monuments in this area.

3. Go through a second gate, past a large standing stone on your left, and then along a line of trees past a white house.

   At the end of the line of trees, follow the yellow arrow on the right

to a gate. Go through the gate and follow the track round to the
left.

4. Continue to the corner of the walls and follow the signpost
straight on.

To your left is a row of stones. Where these meet the track, you can
see a small ring of five stones, just before a yellow arrow. This is a
small stone circle, which had a central pit containing quartz stones
(important in the Bronze Age). If you look ahead, you can clearly see
the Druids' Circle on the skyline.

Go down the main track until you cross a small boggy stream.

To your right are the Penmaenmawr Quarries, which produce much
of Britain's railway ballast! The rock is extremely hard and has been
quarried here since Neolithic times. In the hillside just before the
quarries, is a small rocky outcrop – this was the Graiglwyd
Neolithic axe factory. The rock here breaks with a curved (concoidal)
fracture, which produces very sharp edges, similar to flint. However,
this rock is much harder than flint and made excellent axe heads,
which have been found all over Britain.

Cross the stream and turn left straight up the hill parallel to the
stream. Join a grassy track, which heads up to the circle. Just
before the top of the ridge, take the left branch of the track. Cross a
second boggy patch. Pull or carry up a very short, steep section
(awkward!) to the Druids' Circle.

The Druids' Circle is a famous ring of large stones, 23m diameter,
on a low stone embankment. The entrance is to the west.
Excavation revealed cremation burials containing the bones of
young children, who may have been sacrificial victims! The Druids'
Circle is still visited on the Summer Solstice.

Retrace your steps back to the No Entry sign. Carry on down the
track, round the hillside and back to the car park.

In the area:

The Smallest House (01492 593429) on the quayside in Conwy is Britain's smallest residence. The one-up one-down house was inhabited until 1900. It measures only 6ft wide and 10ft high, and its last resident was over 6ft tall!

Conwy Butterfly Jungle (www.conwy-butterfly.co.uk) is set in 2000 sq ft of jungle garden and has many of the world's most beautiful tropical butterflies, which you can watch in free flight with full rainforest surround sound. There is a souvenir shop, refreshments and picnic area.

Walk 7: Sychnant Pass, Conwy

Allow: *2 hours 30 minutes*

Sychnant Pass lies at the western end of Conwy Mountain and affords spectacular views to Anglesey to the west and the Conwy Valley to the east. From Conwy Mountain you can look out across the sea to Llandudno and Great Orme.

This walk takes you on gravel tracks, country roads and grassy paths along the flanks of Conwy Mountain and through the surrounding countryside. You pass through open moorland, deciduous woods and farmland, and you may see wild horses and buzzards en route. There is a ladder stile; however this can be avoided if walking solo via a short stretch of road.

Map: Ordnance Survey 1:25000 Explorer OL17 – grid reference 750770

Distance: 3½ miles (6km)

Getting there: From the centre of either Conwy or Penmaenmawr follow the signs to Sychnant. Park in the car park at the western end of the walled road.

From the car park head north up the signposted tarmac track.

> To the west you can see the rounded profile of Foel Lus (Walk 6) and Anglesey.

At the junction at the top of the hill, turn right along the broad gravel track. Stay on the track as it curves round to the right, ignoring small paths off to the left.

> You may see wild ponies on the hills around here.

Turn right at the footpath sign before a farm, cross the small stream by the ford (sometimes boggy) and take the right-hand fork heading uphill on a broad gravel track.

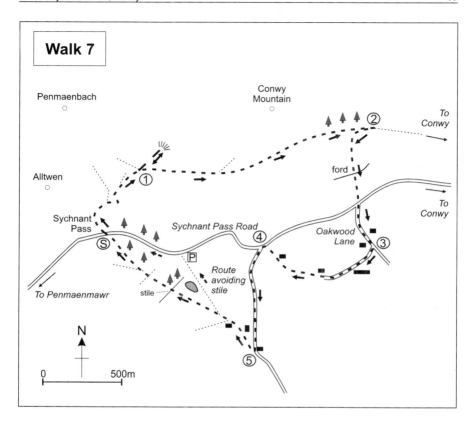

Ahead you can see Conwy Mountain, and to your left are some old quarry workings. The top of Conwy Mountain is the site an Iron Age hill-fort, Castell Caer Lleion.

1. Head down hill to a cross-roads. Take the grassy track straight ahead to see spectacular views across the bay to Great Orme and Llandudno and, in clear weather, the Lake District and Isle of Man.

Retrace your steps to the cross-roads. Turn left to rejoin the main track and head along the track with a stone wall on your right-hand side.

Follow the track round to the right (can be boggy in wet weather) and continue downhill.

There are good views up the Conwy Valley to your right and straight ahead you can see Conwy, Conwy castle and the Conwy estuary.

The path levels out after a loose rocky stretch and you pass through oak woodland. A track can be seen below you to your right.

2. Continue until the two tracks meet and turn sharp right to double back along the lower track. Follow the track round to the left and go through a gate. Carry on along the track, crossing a small stream by a footbridge next to a ford.

    On reaching the road, cross over and take the small lane opposite (Oakwood Lane). Go down the lane until you see a large timber-framed house on the right (Crow's Nest Hall).

3. Turn right immediately before this house and its ornate gate-posts. A footpath sign is hidden in the hedge. Continue along the lane between the buildings, bearing round to the left into open countryside. Ignore footpath signs to the left.

    The road ends at a house called "Inglewood". Pass between the white house gate and a metal field gate to follow the narrow foot-path between two walls to the left of the house.

    Go through a gate next to a ladder stile into a meadow and pass the houses through two more gates to meet a small road. Turn right and go to the end of the road.

    Note, the picnic table belongs to the house and is not for public use!

4. Turn left onto the main road and immediately left again, sign-posted "Berthlwyd Hall Hotel". Continue along the road for about 500m until you pass a large house on your right. Just after the house is a small grassy track doubling back to the right with a "No cars" and a footpath sign.

5. Turn sharp right up this track and continue behind the house. The path steepens and bears left. Continue up the hill until you reach "The Lodge".

Conwy and Castle

Once past the house turn right and head downhill towards a small lake. Do not take the track straight ahead.

Turn left down a grassy path just before the lake. Walk round the far side of the lake heading for a ladder stile on a wall. (To avoid the ladder stile continue down the main gravel track, go round the wooden barrier and past a car park to the main road. Turn left and continue on the road which runs between high stone walls, watching out for traffic as there is no verge. The car park is at the end of the walls.)

Lift the pushchair over the ladder stile. Continue uphill along a small path with a wall to your right. Continue to follow the wall downhill to a concrete water tank, taking care of the drop-off to your right. The path is narrow and slightly awkward here.

Carry straight on, following the wall, ignoring paths to your left and right. At the second junction follow the yellow arrow straight on. Continue down the path until you reach a gate. Go through the gate to find your car and enjoy the view! There is often an ice-cream van in the car park.

In the area:

Conwy Castle and Town Walls (www.conwy.com) date from the time of Edward I in 1283. Conwy is a classic walled town, built by the English in an attempt to contain the Welsh. After visiting the castle, you can walk round the town walls, but keep children under control as there are steep drops.

Pinewood Stables (01492 592256), located on the road between Sychnant and Conwy, offer pony trekking for novices and experienced riders in the countryside and beaches around Conwy. All rides are accompanied by an experienced leader.

Walk 8: Llyn Crafnant, Trefriw

Allow: *2 hours 30 minutes*

Llyn Crafnant is a picturesque lake nestling in a valley surrounded by rugged hills and forest. The views around the lake are spectacular and there is even a café en route! There are no water sports on the lake as it is a reservoir, and this adds to its tranquillity.

This is an easy walk around the lake shore, mainly on forest tracks and quiet roads. However, there is a short stretch of rough path which may require some lifting.

Map: Ordnance Survey 1:25000 Explorer OL17 – grid reference 756618

Distance: 2½ miles (4km)

Getting there: To reach Llyn Crafnant, take the B5106 to Trefriw and follow the signs from the centre of the village. Drive up the valley, past houses and old mine workings (to your left). Park in the forestry commission car park (small fee), where there are toilets and picnic tables.

Leave the car park via the road entrance to avoid six steps. Turn right to walk along the road with the River Crafnant on your right-hand side. At the obelisk, pause to admire the view down the lake towards the jagged Crimpiau hills.

The hills round here are the remains of volcanoes which erupted about 450 million years ago. Don't worry, there's not much chance of an eruption now!

1. Turn right off the road, lifting the pushchair over a locked gate. Head along the forestry track which follows the lake shore.

There is access to the lake shore and small pebbly beaches along the track, but be aware that swimming is not allowed due to the use of the lake as a reservoir.

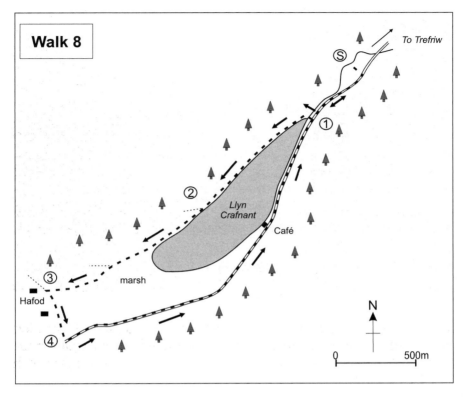

2. At the next junction, take the left fork to continue along the lake shore. The track gets bumpy by a waterfall for about 20m.

   Look out for the old mine workings on the opposite lake shore. These were a slate mine (disused by 1896) and a small slate quarry (closed in 1920).

   Carry on along the track, as the end of the lake turns into marshy reed beds. This shows that the land was once part of the lake but is now silted up.

   You may be lucky enough to see adders on the track, but if you do don't disturb them!

   The path heads up hill and becomes narrow and very rocky. It is still pushable, but it may be easier to carry over short stretches.

Llyn Crafnant and Crimpiau

3. At the junction, marked with a yellow arrow on a post, turn left downhill to a stream and a ladder stile (avoidable via a gap in the fence). You will need to carry the pushchair down a rough stretch of about 50m.

Pause before the stile for a rest and to look at the waterfall to your right.

Go past the ladder stile, where the path becomes even again with tree roots. Continue past a house (Hafod) and over a wooden footbridge (two steps at either end).

A hafod was a summer farmstead, often in the hills, where the family moved with animals for summer grazing.

At the end of the footbridge, turn left through a gate, away from the house, and head down the road. Carry on straight ahead, ignoring drives to your right, until you reach the road junction marked with a yellow post.

4. Turn left, through another gate, and head along the metalled road, back along the opposite lake shore.

About half way along the lake, there is a café serving coffee, teas, lunches and ice cream! Look for the fish beds in the lake here, used to breed trout for fishing.

Carry on along the road until you reach the obelisk once more.

The obelisk commemorates the donation of the lake, surrounding land and a cottage, by Richard James Esq. of Llanrwst in 1896.

Pass the obelisk and continue back along the road to the car park.

In the area:

Llyn Geirionydd: Swimming, waterskiing, canoeing and windsurfing are allowed on this lake, which is signposted from the B5106 near Llanrwst. There are also picnic areas, and the road along the eastern shore is walkable with a pushchair!

The Alice in Wonderland Centre in Llandudno (www.wonderland.co.uk) has a walk-through Wonderland Rabbit Hole with life-sized animated displays of some of the most well known scenes from the Alice story. Visitors are provided with a personal stereo to listen to a narration and sound effects as they walk through the Rabbit Hole. There is also a shop selling Alice related gifts.

Walk 9: Eigiau to Melynllyn, Tal-y-Bont

Allow: *4 hours*

This is an extreme pushchair walk, in a remote location with a truly "Alpine" feel! If you want to do this walk, you should be fit, used to hill walking, and a competent off-roader with a pushchair. It has a prolonged and, at times, steep uphill section and is a long way from civilisation.

Because of this, it is a fantastic, isolated walk, ideal for hill-walkers frustrated by the presence of a pushchair! The walk takes you up a remote valley on the flanks of Carnedd Llewelyn. There are glorious views of the Carneddau ridges and Conwy Valley, and you won't meet many other people!

Map: Ordnance Survey 1:25000 Explorer OL17 – grid reference 732663

Distance: 5 miles (8km)

Getting there: To reach the start of the walk: Drive up the B5106 from Conwy up the Conwy Valley as far as Tal-y-Bont. Take the second turning on the right, which is after the pub (Y Bedol). Continue up a steep, narrow, winding road. Where the road forks, bear right. Go through 2 gates. Park in the car park on the right before the locked gate.

Walk back to the ladder stile and gate at the start of the car park. Lift the pushchair over the gate and walk along the rocky track towards the ridge.

If you look up the valley to the left, you can see the remains of the Llyn Eigiau dam, built to provide the aluminium works in Dolgarrog with hydro-electricity. This dam breached catastrophically on 2˙ November 1925, flooding the village in the valley below and killing 16 people. The flood destroyed much of the village, including the

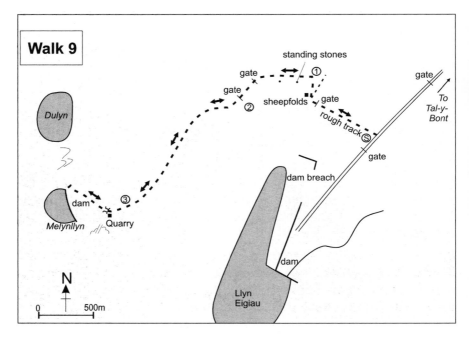

original church, and survivors reported hearing the church bell toll as the building was swept away.

Pass through an open gate and follow the track (now grassy) as it zigzags up the ridge. Ignore the track to the right just before the large boulders.

Note the old sheep enclosures to your right.

The path is quite steep and rocky in places and note that there is quite a steep drop to your right as you go uphill.

Here, you get good views of the hills around the Conwy Valley. The middle of the three hills you can see in front of you is Pen-y-Gaer, an Iron Age hill-fort, and you can see the remains of the three ramparts.

1. Continue uphill round to the left, past two standing stones on your left (the first has been used as a gate-post). The track becomes rocky again for about 100m.

Pen yr Helgi Du and Llyn Eigiau

Carry on uphill and through a gate, with views up the valley. The track is rocky again for a short distance.

2. Continue along the track and through a second gate. The track alternates between grassy track and bumpy rocky surface and is rough in places.

   To your right you can see the cliffs leading up to Foel Fras and Garnedd Uchaf. At the base of the cliffs is Dulyn (Black Lake), which has an aeroplane propeller sticking out of its waters. Along the track leading from Dulyn down the other side of the valley, there are also fragments of an aeroplane fuselage. These are the remains of a Whitley Mk.V BD232, which crashed on 26th September 1942 while on a night training flight, killing all 5 crew on board. The plane was found three days later.

3. Go down a short, steep downhill section, which you may need to carry over on the way back.

Just before the track bends to the right to head up to the lake, there is a ruined building to your left. Behind this, in the hillside, is a series of disused quarry workings (Melynllyn Hone Quarry) – a diagonal cut into the hillside, flanked by spoil heaps to its right, and two adit holes within the cut. Inside the building, there are the remains of a winch, a channel for a waterwheel and part of the waterwheel driving mechanism.

Go over a wooden bridge, along the track, now passing diagonally along the dam to reach the lake at its right-hand end.

The hill directly above Melynllyn is Foel Grach, and to its left is Carnedd Llewelyn.

Retrace your steps back to the car park.

In the area:

Trefriw Wells Spa (www.spatone.com): A Victorian pump-room and bath-house at a spa in use since Roman times. Bathing was originally carried out in the Cave of Wells, with the cyclopean bath-house built in 1743. You can tour the caverns and bath-house, try the waters and treat yourself to a cream tea in the café.

Bodnant Gardens (www.bodnantgarden.co.uk) in the beautiful Conwy Valley consists of formal gardens around the house and lower woodland gardens alongside the river. You can explore the gardens along the many paths, most of which are accessible for pushchairs (most steps can be avoided). There is a plant centre and gift shop in the garden and a large tea room next to the car park. Toilets are located in the car park (none in the gardens) and have baby changing facilities.

Walk 10: Gwydyr Forest Mines, Llanrwst

Allow: *1 hour 30 minutes*

Gwydyr is a large area of forest around Betws-y-Coed and Llanrwst, renowned both for its scenic beauty and its mining heritage. There is a myriad of tracks and paths through the forest and the area can be explored over repeated visits.

This walk is a short, easy route round the woodland and mine workings west of Llanrwst, in the Parc and Hafna areas, along back roads, forest tracks and woodland paths. This is a mountain biking forest, and many of the tracks are multi-use, so beware of bikes and other vehicles.

Map: Ordnance Survey 1:25000 Explorer OL17 – grid reference 790609

Distance: 2½ miles (4km)

Getting there: From the B5106, between Trefriw and Llanrwst, turn up the minor road signposted Llyn Geirionydd (there is also a large forestry sign at this junction). Continue to a crossroads. Turn left here into the forestry car park.

From the car park, walk back to the road and turn left. After a few metres, at the next junction turn left down a metalled track signposted to car parks (barrier sometimes locked). Walk up the road past the car park (portaloos here!) with woodland on your left and fields to your right.

> These fields are actually landscaped mine spoil heaps from the Parc mine.

Continue up the road, ignoring bike tracks to your left, and past another yellow and black barrier. Head up the hill and past the first track on the right.

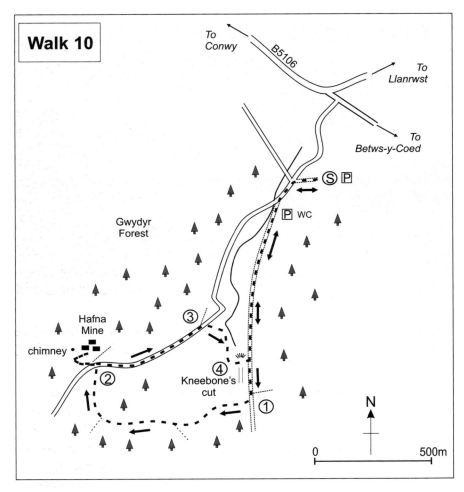

Walk 10

To Conwy

B5106

To Llanrwst

To Betws-y-Coed

Ⓢ Ⓟ

Ⓟ WC

Gwydyr Forest

Hafna Mine

chimney

③

②

④

Kneebone's cut

①

N

0   500m

1. At the next junction, a large cross-roads, turn right down the gravel track. Follow the track as it winds through mixed woodland.

   Pass a large lay-by where the woodland changes to conifers and continue along the main track, ignoring the small path to your left marked with a pick and hammer symbol.

2. At the end of the track, go past a metal barrier and turn left onto the road looking out for traffic. Take the next right, marked with a

Hafna Mine buildings

footpath sign to visit the Hafna Mine. Take the path up hill to your left which gives pushchair access to the lower building levels and an information board.

This is the remains of the Hafna Mine smelting house. Hafna is unique in Gwydyr, in being the only lead mine with its own smelting house. The site has a slime pit (!), now a reed bed, and a large brick chimney which got rid of the toxic lead fumes when smelting was in progress. The buildings can be explored, but keep children under control as it is an old mine working. Small amounts of galena ore can still be found in the gravel around the site – this is shiny dark grey, occurs in white quartz and feels very heavy. It is a lead ore so don't let children chew it! The site is also home to bat colonies, including the rare horseshoe bat. DO NOT DISTURB THE BATS. There is a hefty fine if you do so (£1000 per bat disturbed!).

From Hafna, return to the road and turn left to walk down the road watching out for vehicles and mountain bikes.

3. Continue to a large lay-by with a forest track to the left and a gate on the right into a field. Just below the gate, turn right between two boulders (narrow) and head down a woodland path marked with the pick and hammer symbol.

Immediately beyond the boulders, the path widens. Continue along this path through the forest, past wooden fencing on your left.

Head uphill to a tarmac viewpoint, with views across the landscaped mine workings to the Conwy Valley. There is an information board here on the Parc Mine workings, the largest in Gwydr Forest, recent landscaping and ecology.

The outrun is water from the Parc mine third level on the Principle Lode, one of three major lodes in the area and which extends for 1 ½ miles. The lodes are mineral rich veins found between beds of hard volcanic rock and softer shales. The main mineral mined was lead, with minor zinc also mined. The lead ore here is galena (lead sulphide) and the zinc is found in zinc blende (zinc sulphide). Mining started in this area in the early 1600s and was in its heyday in the mid-1800s.

4. Follow the tarmac path heading left from the viewpoint to look at Kneebone's Cutting, which can be accessed across the stile (signposted) – you will need to either park the pushchair or lift it over the stile, but the cutting is only about 15m away.

Kneebone's Cutting is a large cavern named after the miner "Captain" Kneebone. The cutting is marked on maps of the 1899 mine workings, forming part of the Gors Lode.

From the cutting, continue along the tarmac path to the metalled track you came up at the start of the walk. Turn left down the track, downhill past the car park and back to the road. Turn right onto the road and right again into the car park to find your car.

In the area:

Gwydir Castle (www.gwydir-castle.co.uk) is a Tudor courtyard house in 10 acres of gardens. It is undergoing refurbishment by the present owners who welcome visitors to wander around many of the rooms. There are allegedly ghosts and small children's imaginations will run wild, but keep a close eye on them as floors and steps are uneven.

Conwy River Cruises (www.conwyboats.co.uk) – enjoy a scenic trip or a wildlife cruise up the River Conwy on board one of the Princess Christine cruise boats.

Walk 11: Llyn Elsi, Betws-y-Coed

Allow: *3 hours*

Llyn Elsi lies hidden in woodland above Betws-y-Coed, a picturesque town nestling in the valley bottom. The town has plenty to offer visitors – a variety of shops, pubs, cafés, the Conwy Valley Railway and, of course, walking.

This walk takes you on forest tracks through the southern end of Gwydr Forest to Llyn Elsi. After a steep climb you are rewarded with stunning views over the lake to the Snowdonia mountains and the Conwy and Lledr Valleys.

Map: Ordnance Survey 1:25000 Explorer OL17 and OL18 – grid reference 793564

Distance: 4 miles (6.5km)

Getting there: Park in any of the car parks in Betws-y-Coed and make your way to St Mary's Church on the main road (A5) through the town centre.

Take the road that goes round the back of the church, this is a loop road so you can start at either end. Directly behind the church there is a footpath up the hill, signposted to Llyn Elsi.

> The start of this walk is the hardest part and this is reflected in the grading. The first 15 minutes involves a steep climb but this gradually evens out and the rest of the walk is on broad gravel tracks either on the level or downhill. The paths can be slippery during the autumn leaf fall.

Go round the metal barrier and follow the footpath uphill through the woodland. Keep following this main path ignoring smaller footpaths to the right.

> Look out for the great views over the Conwy valley on the left.

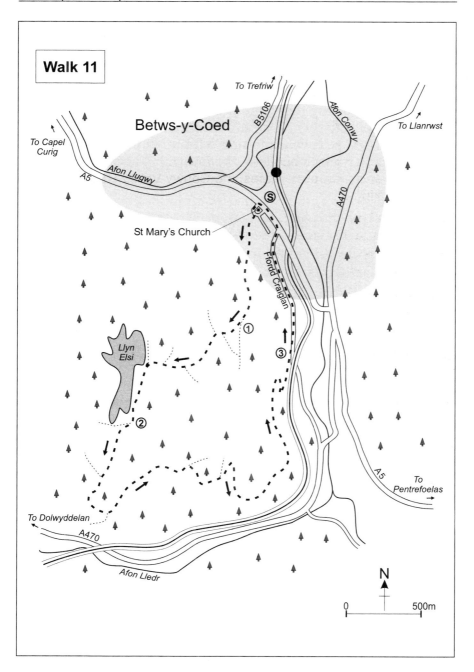

1. After about 25 minutes turn right at a fork in the path. At the next junction turn right again following the white marked posts. Then turn left at the following junction.

   Turn right at the next junction and then left at the junction after that, still following the white posts. Within a few minutes you will see the lake (Llyn Elsi) in front of you. Stop following the white marked path now and turn left so that the lake is on your right. As you walk along there are some fantastic view points over the lake and picnic spots on the right.

2. As you pass the end of the lake continue walking on the main path, ignoring the path on the right. This track brings you down to a metal barrier and then to a junction where you turn left.

   As you go round the bend in this path you will get fantastic views over the Lledr valley.

   At the T-junction turn left and stay on this main path ignoring tracks off to the right and left. When you reach a fork in the road turn right and then right again at the following junction.

   This section of the walk is a steady downhill and there are great views again over the Conwy valley.

3. This track takes you all the way down to a quiet country lane (Ffordd Craiglan) with the railway running alongside. Turn left onto the lane and follow this back to Betws-y-Coed.

   This road is bordered by woodland and is lined with heavily scented wild garlic in spring.

   The lane leads you down to the main road (A5) which passes through Betws-y-Coed so turn left and head into town to find your car.

   At the end of the lane is the outdoor shop 'Rock Bottom' where there is a great little café equipped with high chairs.

In the area:

The Conwy Falls (www.conwy-falls.co.uk) are situated in a Site of Special Scientific Interest a few miles down the A5 towards

Llyn Elsi

Llangollen. There is a small entry fee and the area offers spectacular waterfalls and woodland walks (not all suitable for pushchairs). Along the river you could see otters, ducklings, dippers and even crested newts. There is also a licensed café, which welcomes "well-behaved" children!

Model Railway Museum

(www.snowdonia-information.co.uk/local-attractions/conwyrail.htm) can be found at Betws-y-Coed station in the Old Goods Yard. There are displays on the railways of North Wales, including railway stock and memorabilia. There are working model railway layouts, and you can go for a ride on a steam-hauled miniature railway in the grounds or take the 15-inch-gauge tramway to the woods. There is a model shop and gift shop, café, buffet coach restaurant and picnic area. For children there are self-drive mini dodgems, Postman Pat, school bus and Toby Tram.

Walk 12: Artists' Wood, Miners' Bridge and Swallow Falls, Betws-y-Coed

Allow: *3 hours*

The forest along the Afon Llugwy, west of Betws-y-Coed is known as "Artists' Wood" due to the popularity of the area to Victorian artists who came to paint the beauty spots around Betws-y-Coed. Artists who visited the area include J.M.W. Turner and David Cox, who founded an artists' colony in the town.

This is a hard, long walk on tracks and rugged paths through woodland with some very rough terrain and is not suitable for very small babies.

Map: Ordnance Survey 1:25000 Explorer OL17 – grid reference 762576

Distance: 5 miles (8.5km)

Getting there: Park at Cae'n-y-Coed car park on the A5 between Betws-y-Coed and Capel Curig (forestry commission, small fee). The car park has toilets and picnic tables.

From the car park, turn right up the track signposted to another car park. Take the right-hand fork heading uphill. Go up a grassy track on your left – this is opposite a red marker post.

Cross the path marked with red posts and head for the gate on the skyline. Go through the small gate and into a field. Follow the path across the field towards a gate leading to a grey house called "Hafodty".

1. Go through the gate, turn right to go round the back of the house and through an old wooden gate to the left of an outbuilding.

   Looking back you can see the Crimpiau hills above Llyn Crafnant (Walk 8), and straight ahead you will see the Conwy Valley.

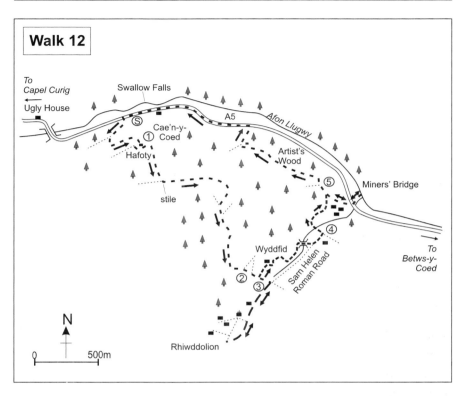

Follow the path to the left diagonally uphill behind the house until you see an old barn. Go through the gate to the left of the barn, marked by a yellow arrow. Follow the track and the yellow arrows across the field to a stone bridge and a stile. Lift over the stile and turn left onto a broad forest track.

At the next junction, follow the track as it bends round to the left and slightly downhill. Carry straight on at the second junction, ignoring the left turn.

2. At the triangular track junction, turn right. To visit Rhiwddolion, continue along the track to a junction on a left-hand bend. Turn right here and follow the road uphill. Go past a white house and through a gate to its left.

When you reach a gate into a field on your right, you can look across into the ruined village of Rhiwddolion.

Continue up the road, following it round to the right, ignoring a gate on the left with a "No Cycles" sign. Carry on into Rhiwddolion and wander along the tracks round the ruined buildings.

This was once a quarry village housing the workers of the Bwlch Gwyn quarry in the woods just to the north. As you explore you will see the ruins of terraces, detached houses and stables. The village was linked to the chapel by a slate flagged path (just pushchairable!). Three of the houses, including the chapel, have been acquired by the Landmark Trust and renovated as holiday accommodation.

Retrace your steps back to the forest road.

3. Turn left onto the track and take a gate into a field on your right before you reach the triangular junction once more. This leads to a grassy track across the field which goes downhill to a white house, "Wyddfid".

Turn right just before the house to follow the track through outbuildings. Go through the gate into the next field, which can be overgrown in summer. Stay close to the wall, following the path round the bend. This section can be boggy!

Join a narrow stony path with loose rocks, which zigzags downhill through woodland. Follow the path along a small stream to a stone footbridge. Cross the bridge and lift the pushchair over a gate. Follow the small path onto a rocky track. Turn left down the track and past a house.

This track, which crosses the river at the Miners' Bridge, is the route of the Roman Road, Sarn Helen, also seen at Trawsfynydd in Walk 19.

4. At the next cross-roads, turn left onto a broad forest track, cross the river and follow the track round to the right.

To the right by a stream you can see impressively tall trees, with very long straight trunks!

Ruined houses, Rhiwddolion

Keep going down the track ignoring small paths to the right. At the large junction of tracks, turn right downhill. Join a metalled road and continue past the houses to the main road.

Cross the road, looking out for traffic, and head through the wooden gate to have a look at the Miners' Bridge.

This unusual bridge over the river Llugwy is a steep, wooden ladder, crossed by the miners on their way to work in the mines of Gwydyr Forest. The bridge is also the site of the earlier Roman crossing for Sarn Helen. There are impressive views of the river and this is a suitable spot to break the walk for a picnic!

Cross the road back to the houses and take the track to the right and uphill. At the first junction, continue on the main track until you see a track to the right marked with a black and white barrier.

5. Turn down this track (look out for cyclists!) and walk through the forest, Artists' Wood, ignoring tracks to the left.

Go past the forestry yard on your right and past a metal barrier, turning right down the track which will bring you back to the main road. Cross the road and turn left to walk along the pavement until you reach the Swallow Falls Hotel.

Tea, coffee, food, bars, a fudge kitchen and children's playground can be found here.

To view the Swallow Falls, go through the turnstile (small fee) or ask to take the pushchair through the gate.

Swallow Falls are one of the beauty spots of North Wales. The name is actually a mis-translation of the Welsh name Rhaeadr Ewynnol (Foaming Falls) which was translated as Rhaeadr-y-Wennol (Swallow Falls). The stream is broken up by rocks into a series of white-water rapids before cascading into a deep chasm. There are benches and viewpoints overlooking the falls, which are particularly impressive after heavy rain.

Continue along the main road for another 300m until you return to the car park.

In the area:

Conwy Valley Railway: the railway runs from Betws-y-Coed to Llandudno and Blaenau Ffestiniog. It is worth taking a ride on the train on a clear day up to Blaenau just for the scenery. Also at the railway station is the Conwy Valley Railway Museum with a miniature railway, shop and restaurant in an old buffet coach.

The Ugly House: Located towards Capel Curig, is the Ugly House (Ty Hyll, www.snowdonia-society.org.uk). It is so named because of the large boulders used in its walls. According to legend, the house was built in 1475 by two outlaw brothers. It was a "Ty Un Nos" (House of One Night). It was said that whoever could build a house overnight and have smoke coming from the chimney by dawn could claim the land it stood on freehold. The boundary of his land could also be extended by the distance that he could throw his axe from the four corners of the new house.

Walk 13: Woodland Walk, Capel Curig

Allow: 1 hour

Capel Curig is situated in the heart of Snowdonia and is a walkers' paradise, with mountain access, woodland, rivers, pubs and outdoor shops. From the south-west end of the village there are views down the valley to the Snowdon Horseshoe and Carnedd Moel Siabod towers above the road to the south.

This short walk takes you through woodland on the lower flanks of Carnedd Moel Siabod, generally on easy tracks with a short section on steep forest paths.

Map: Ordnance Survey 1:25000 Explorer OL17 – grid reference 727579

Distance: 2 miles (3.5km)

Getting there: When driving through Capel Curig on the A5 in the direction of Betws-y-Coed take the turning opposite the petrol station. This is signposted to a parking area. Leave your car in one of the parking spots on the left.

Walk up the track away from the road. Go through the wooden gateposts ahead; don't take the path to the right. When you come to a T-junction take the right-hand path. This leads you almost immediately to a fork in the track where you take the left-hand path up the hill. This is a steady climb up hill for around 20 minutes.

As the road levels out you will come to another junction. Take the right-hand path straight ahead, not the left-hand path up the hill.

1. As the path begins to head downhill you will cross a small stream. Take the narrow rocky track on the right immediately after this, which looks much worse than it is!

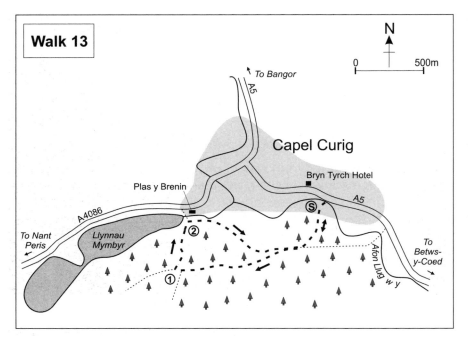

This track heads through woodland and has several rocky sections but as it is downhill it is relatively easy to negotiate.

Just before you enter pine forest, you get a spectacular view across to Snowdon and the Glyders to your left.

2. The path leads you down to a crossroads with the outdoor centre, Plas-y-Brenin, and the lakes in front of you.

If you take a very short detour down to the footbridge ahead you will be rewarded with spectacular views across the lakes (Llynnau Mymbyr) to the Snowdon horseshoe.

Turn right and walk along the track with the lake on your left.

As you walk along this path you will see a large hill, Craig Wen, on your left.

After 5 minutes you will pass through a gateway (there is a small gate alongside this if the main gate is closed).

The buildings on your left are Bryn Engan, an outdoor centre.

The Snowdon Horseshoe and Llynnau Mymbyr

After a further 20 minutes, you come to a junction (the path on the right that goes up the hill is the route we followed at the start of the walk). Go straight ahead here and at the next junction take the left-hand path. You soon come to the end of the walk and your car.

In the area:

Caernarfon Castle (www.cadw.wales.gov.uk) is one of the world's greatest medieval castles and certainly the most striking medieval monument in Wales. The castle was constructed in 1283 by Edward I not only as a military stronghold but also as a royal palace. Its unique polygonal towers and colour-banded walls, as well as its sheer size, make it a spectacular place to visit. The castle is open every month except December and January and has a great museum and eagle and dragon audio-visual display.

Gypsy Wood Park (www.gypsywood.co.uk) is the largest LGB garden railway in Wales. There are lots of miniature animals, a touch and smell garden, wetland walk and small children's play area. It is open between Easter and mid-September 10.30am-5.00pm.

Walk 14: Riverside Walk, Beddgelert

Allow: 1 hour

This is a gentle walk on metalled paths, stony tracks and across grass. It follows the banks of the River Glaslyn from the picturesque village of Beddgelert in the heart of Snowdonia. As well as woodland and meadows along the riverbanks and the remnants of copper mining in the Glaslyn valley, on a clear day you will see Snowdon. The walk also visits Gelert's Grave, site of a local legend.

The tourist information centre can be found at the entrance to the car park. The village has a selection of cafés and pubs, gift shops, a general store and an outdoor shop.

Map: Ordnance Survey 1:25 000 Explorer OL17 – grid reference 589482

Distance: 2 miles (3.2km)

Getting there: Head for the centre of the village. Parking is limited near the river, but a Pay and Display car park is located on the A498 to Porthmadog, near the Royal Goat Hotel.

From the car park, turn left past the Tourist Information and head towards the village centre. Where the road bends to go over a bridge, continue straight ahead to follow the right-hand river bank, keeping the National Trust's "Ty Isaf" on your right.

> This cottage was previously known as Bwthyn Llywelyn and is the oldest house in the village.

Go past the public toilets to a footbridge over the river.

1. Cross the bridge and turn immediately right to follow a metalled path down the river bank. Just before the first gate, there is a picnic site with tables and benches.

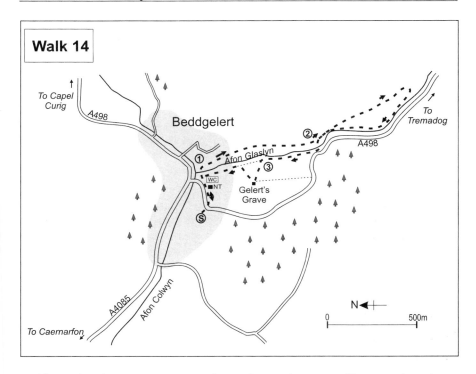

Note the decorative gates along the path — you will see a church window, a train and two fish!

Continue along the wooded riverbank. After the second gate, the path joins the line of the old railway.

On the hillside to your left you can see spoil heaps and adit entrances, the remains of once industrious copper mining in the area. The hillside is now covered with deciduous woodland and abundant rhododendrons. Though attractive when covered in purple flowers, rhododendrons are a problem in this area as they colonise the land, depriving it of nutrients essential for indigenous species. Rhododendrons have no natural consumers and are notoriously difficult to destroy.

2. At the bridge, do not cross the river yet, but turn left down a gravel track.

The walk can be shortened here by crossing the bridge, turning right and heading straight back to the village via Gelert's grave (see instruction number 3).

Follow the path until you see an information board on your right-hand side, with the title "Aberglaslyn". Turn right past the board to follow the river bank down a grassy path (through bracken in summer), with shaded grassy spots for picnics and pebbly beaches for paddling.

The grassy path rejoins the track, turn left here and head back towards the bridge. NB The path along this stretch is rocky.

The railway does continue to the right here, but the path stops at a barrier. Pedestrians can follow the river down to the Pass of Aberglaslyn, but this is not suitable for pushchairs and is even somewhat adventurous for papooses!

Cross over the bridge and turn immediately right up the opposite river bank, along a metalled path back towards the village.

3. After the third gate, opposite a water pumping station, turn left up a path heading towards a small stone enclosure. This enclosure contains a bronze statue of Gelert, the dog of the Beddgelert legend. With your back to the enclosure, head left towards the village and church. Beneath two trees, you will come to Gelert's Grave, a rough gravestone with the legend written on a bronze plaque:

In the 13th century Llywelyn, prince of North Wales, had a palace at Beddgelert. One day he went hunting without Gelert, the faithful hound, who was unaccountably absent. On Llywelyn's return the truant, stained and smeared with blood, joyfully sprang to meet his master. The prince, alarmed, hastened to find his son, and saw the infant's cot empty, the bedclothes and floor covered with blood. The frantic father plunged his sword into the hound's side, thinking it had killed his heir. The dog's dying yell was answered by a child's cry. Llywelyn searched and discovered his boy unharmed, but near by lay the body of a mighty wolf which Gelert had slain. The prince, filled with remorse, is said never to have smiled again. He buried Gelert here. The spot is called Beddgelert.

Gelert's grave and Beddgelert

The path rejoins the river bank, turn left back to the bridge in the village, past the toilets (no changing facilities) and retrace your steps to the car park.

In the area:

Sygun Copper Mine (www.syguncoppermine.co.uk) north of Beddgelert, offers a spectacular underground audio-visual experience. You can tour the Victorian caverns, decorated with stalactites and stalagmites. Other activities include nature trails, pottery painting, gold-panning, archery, coin making, trampolining and there is a café and adventure playground.

The Fun Centre (Y Hwylfan, www.thefuncentre.co.uk), Caernarfon, offers a variety of fun activities for all the family – ball pools, rope bridges, slides, cargo nets and much more. As well as games for the Big Kids, there are 2 large play areas for under-5s with seating. There is also a café and baby changing facilities

Walk 15: Llyn Mair, Maentwrog

Allow: 1 hour

Llyn Mair is a picturesque lake in the Vale of Ffestiniog, east of Porthmadog. The woodland surrounding the lake is part of an old Welsh rainforest, and contains a habitat found only on the western edge of Europe.

This is an easy walk, following stony tracks through the woodland along the edge of the lake. It's also close to the Ffestiniog Railway, and this walk can be combined with a trip by steam train to Tan-y-Bwlch station, which makes an alternative start point.

Map: Ordnance Survey 1:25000 Explorer OL18 – grid reference 652413

Distance: 1½ miles (3km)

Getting there: Park in the car park next to the lake (Llyn Mair) on the B4410. This is just down the road from the Tan-y-Bwlch train station, which has a cafe selling hot and cold food and ice creams. It also has high chairs and baby changing facilities.

This walk can also be reached on foot from the train station, just head down the hill, turn left on to the road and walk along until you find the first car park on the left.

Leave the car park and cross the road. Go through the gateway and you will see the lake and a grassy picnic area on your left. Follow the gravel path down towards the right.

1. After 5 minutes you will come to a junction marked on a wooden post as number 26. Turn left down the smaller path which leads you around the lake. As you follow the path along you will enter the Coed Hafod-y-Llyn woodland.

    Trees in the woodland include oak, ash and birch with luxuriant mosses. Look out for green woodpeckers, blue tits, nuthatches, buzzards, woodwarblers and flycatchers.

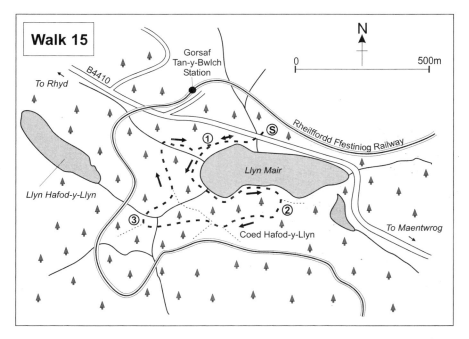

Continue past a small pond on your right, surrounded by bamboo, and continue along the edge of the lake.

In summer the lake is partially covered with water lilies.

2. Part way round the lake you will come to a junction (number 10). Turn right through the gateway. The track is a little bumpy as you go up a series of short uphill stretches but the terrain soon evens out.

As the path levels out you will come to another junction (number 9). Go through the gateway straight ahead. Almost immediately the path splits again (number 8). Take the right-hand path, not the left which leads you up to a railway crossing, though this is a good viewpoint for watching the steam trains!

As you head down the path you will come to a clearing next to a stream with a couple of benches which is a nice spot to stop for a break.

3. The path leads you to another junction (number 28) where you turn right down the hill along a broad gravel track. At the next junction (number 27) turn left.

You will come across a great view point with a bench on the right from which you can see across the lake to the hill Moelwyn Bach.

Follow this main path along, ignoring any turnings to the left and right, and it will bring you back to the start point next to the lake and picnic site. So go through the gate, cross the road and find your car in the car park.

Llyn Mair woodland

In the area:

The Ffestiniog Railway (www.festrail.co.uk) is a narrow gauge steam railway running along the Vale of Ffestiniog from Porthmadog to Blaenau Ffestiniog. It is the oldest independent railway company in the world and runs steam trains throughout the summer months and a combination of diesel and steam the rest of the year. There are special children's events throughout the year and a "Talking Train" runs daily at noon, giving you stories and information about the area. Porthmadog and Tan-y-Bwlch Stations have cafés with highchairs and baby changing facilities.

Blackrock Sands is located on the western outskirts Porthmadog. The beach stretches for miles and is a haven for beach games and resting.

Walk 16: Hafod-y-Llyn to Llyn Trefor, Maentwrog

Allow: 1 hour 30 minutes

Hafod-y-Llyn and Llyn Trefor are two lakes in the Vale of Ffestiniog, in woodland to the west of Llyn Mair (Walk 15). The woodland is a mixture of deciduous Welsh rainforest habitat and coniferous plantation.

The walk is initially on broad forest tracks round the lakes, with a short adventurous climb through forest paths on your return. There are views over the Vale of Ffestiniog and the Ffestiniog Railway, and down to Portmeirion and the estuary at Porthmadog.

Map: Ordnance Survey 1:25000 Explorer OL18 – grid reference 646416

Distance: 2½ miles (4km)

Getting there: Park in the woodland car park just up the road (B4410) from Tan-y-Bwlch station. (This walk can also be reached on foot from the train station, just head down the hill, turn right on to the road, pass under the railway bridge and walk along until you find the first car park on the left).

Go through the kissing gate at the end of the car park and follow the track along. After a few minutes you will see the lake (Llyn Hafod-y-Llyn) ahead of you. Take the small path on the left just before the lake. Follow this path along the side of the lake and through a small area of woodland.

There is a lovely picnic spot at the far end of the lake.

1. At the end of the lake turn left off this small path onto the main track. Stay on this main track ignoring paths off it until you come to a junction (marked on a wooden post with the number 7). Take the right-hand fork to continue straight ahead. You will soon

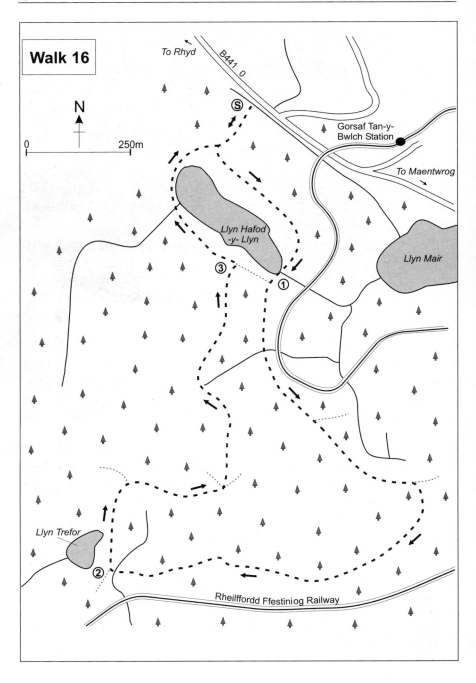

Walk 16

N

0   250m

To Rhyd

B441 0

Ⓢ

Gorsaf Tan-y-
Bwlch Station

To Maentwrog

Llyn Hafod
-y- Llyn

Llyn Mair

③

①

Rheilffordd Ffestiniog Railway

Llyn Trefor

②

Tan-y-Bwlch station

come to another junction (number 6) where you also take the right-hand fork.

On the left of this track you can see great views over the Vale of Ffestiniog at the base of which is the river Afon Dwyryd. At the end of the estuary you can see Tremadog Bay.

2. The path then passes the lake, Llyn Trefor on the left. Soon after you pass the lake you will come to a junction (number 19). Turn right here and follow the small path up into the woodland. This path is narrow in places, but relatively easy to negotiate with the pushchair. You will soon enter some denser woodland and follow the path up the left-hand edge.

You will be able to see a stone wall on the right. The track can be steep in places and involves pushing the pushchair over some tree roots but it soon levels out.

You will soon arrive at a crossroads (number 18). Go straight across and the track soon broadens.

There are great views of the hill Moelwyn Bach on the right.

3. This path ends in a short but steep downhill section. This brings you down to a stone hut. Turn left just before the hut and left again to rejoin the main track that runs alongside Llyn Hafod-y-Llyn.

   As you walk back along this track with the lake on your right you will see some benches and picnic spots. Continue along the track until you reach the car park.

In the area:

Portmeirion is an Italianate village created between 1926 to 1976 by the architect Clough Williams-Ellis on his own private peninsula (www.portmeirion-village.com). It is the origin of Portmeirion pottery and was the setting for the TV series "The Prisoner". You can have an intriguing day out wandering round the buildings and browsing in the small shops. You can also walk through pretty subtropical gardens and woodland (easy paths) on the shore of the estuary and walk on the extensive sandy beach (tide times are shown on all entry tickets). Most of the village is accessible by push-chair, though there are some steps. There is a café and toilets with baby changing facilities. Dogs are not allowed in the village.

The Welsh Highland Railway (www.whr.co.uk) runs from Portmadog to Caernarfon and provides a good family day out. A trip on the narrow gauge railway includes a visit to the engine sheds and a chance to climb on the engines and watch the signals and points being changed. There is a shop and café with children's menu.

Walk 17: Rhaeadr Cynfal, Llanffestiniog

Allow: 1 hour

Rhaeadr Cynfal is a picturesque waterfall tumbling down a rocky gorge at the bottom of a wooded valley. The deciduous trees surrounding the river are the remnant of an ancient woodland, and home to an abundance of mosses, lichens and liverworts.

The waterfall is easily accessible from the village of Llanffestiniog on the A470, and this is a relatively easy walk down tracks through farmland and woods. There is a flight of easy steps to the waterfall and some stamina will be needed for the uphill push back to the village.

Map: Ordnance Survey 1:25000 Explorer OL18 – grid reference 700419

Distance: 1½ miles (2.5km)

Getting there: Park in Llanffestiniog by the church.

With your back to the church turn left down the main road (A470). Stay on the main road; do not take the left turn to Blaenau Ffestiniog. Go past the post office and shop, and continue until you see a railway bridge and a sign to Dolgellau/Bala.

1. Just before the railway bridge, take the right turn down a lane, signposted "Rhaeadr Cynfal Falls". Go down the lane following it to the left and through a gate. Follow the road as it bends right past the house "Clogwyn Brith".

   Go through a gate to the left of the large barn and then through a second gate. This takes you to a broad track between two fences with woodland on your left.

2. At the end of the track, just before a barn, follow the sign to the falls and take the left-hand wooden gate into a field. The path is a broad grassy track at the top of open fields following the fence.

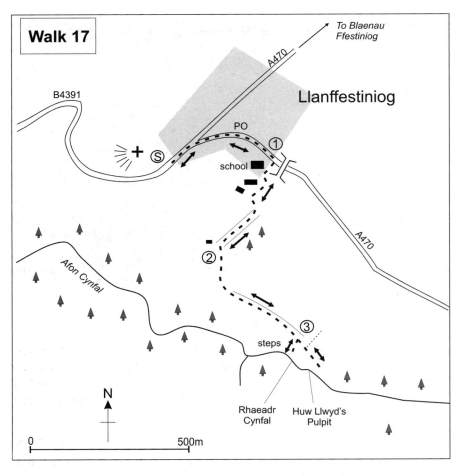

To your right you can see the Ffestiniog Valley and Tan-y-Bwlch woodland (Walks 15 and 16).

Pass through a gate into the next field. Go along the top of the field with a wall on your left and a steep grassy slope dropping off to your right. The pushchair leash is advisable on this part of the walk.

In the valley below you can see the broad-leafed woodland surrounding the river. This woodland is the remnants of an ancient woodland that used to cover most of Wales. Many of the plants and animals can only thrive in a damp atmosphere with old trees, and in autumn there are beautiful leaf colours.

Pass two walls and head downhill to a narrow wooden gate.

3. Go through the gate and take the right fork down a path with shallow steps (signposted). Take the pushchair down the steps; though there are

Which way now?

75 steps (!) they are shallow and easy!

Park the pushchair by the fence at the top of the steep stone steps (unsuitable for pushchairs). The waterfall can be viewed from a viewing platform down these steps, or over the fence to the left of the steps. The waterfall is visible without losing sight of your baby if you are solo.

Head back up the steps; backwards is easiest and the top 20 are avoidable by heading up the grass to the side. At the top, turn right along the level woodland path.

As you get a clear view down into the river, you can see a square pillar of rock in the centre of the river. This is Huw Llwyd's Pulpit.

Huw Llwyd of Cynfal was a famous Welsh poet, mercenary, soothsayer and sorcerer (c.1568-c.1630) and was allegedly the seventh son of a seventh son. There are many stories about him, among which he is said to have defeated two witches who took the form of cats, charmed the birds from the trees and taught the devil about tobacco. Those who crossed him were sorely punished. His pulpit in the Afon Cynfal was used to deliver nocturnal addresses and incantations, and to exorcise people plagued with demons.

In spite of the tales he was a real person and probably used the legends to enforce his authority in this area. He was a soldier in the army of King James I and travelled as a mercenary in Europe. While on his travels he wrote books on military strategy, astronomical lore, astrological charts and healing plants, which probably led to his reputation as a sorcerer.

Head back to the top of the steps and follow the same route back to the village and your car. If the weather is clear, the viewpoint down the path to the left of the church is strongly recommended!

In the area:

Llechwedd Slate Caverns in Blaenau Ffestiniog (www.llechwedd-slate-caverns.co.uk) offer an insight into the slate mining industry in the area. Travel down the miners' tramway for a multimedia tour of the vast underground caverns. There is a Victorian village at the surface with shops, a pub, workshop exhibits and slate dressing demonstrations.

Maes Artro Living History Museum in Llanbedr (www.maesartro.co.uk), houses a collection of planes and memorabilia from the war and local rural life in the past. It is set in grounds with a woodland nature trail, picnic areas and children's play areas. The restaurant has a healthy kids' menu or you could indulge them in the ice cream parlour! Opening is limited in winter.

Walk 18: Lake and Riverside, Bala

Allow: 1 hour

This is an easy urban saunter along riverside and lakeside paths. Bala was once known for its woollen goods and is now an international centre for water sports. Llyn Tegid (Bala Lake) is the largest lake in Wales and the Rheilffordd Llyn Tegid (Bala Lake Railway) runs down the whole length of the eastern shore. This walk can either be done from the car park or from the train station.

The famous legend connected with Bala is that of Mary Jones who saved for several years to buy a bible. In 1880, on hearing that Thomas Charles the great Welsh revivalist was in town, she walked 25 miles barefoot to buy one only to find he had sold them all. He was so impressed with her dedication that he gave her his own. This legend is thought to have inspired the founding of the British and Foreign Bible Society.

Map: Ordnance Survey 1:25000 Explorer OL23 – grid reference 929361

Distance: 2 miles (4km)

Getting there: Park in the car park next to the recycle centre. This is just off the A494, opposite the turning for the A4212. There are toilets in the car park and a children's playground next door.

Walk towards the recycling point and between some wooden railings to the riverside path. Turn right through the kissing gate and walk along the grassy path, away from the bridge with the river (Afon Tryweryn) on your left.

There are lovely views of the surrounding hills.

As you walk along the path you will pass a weir on your left and soon you will come to kissing gate. Turn right, cross over the tarmac lane and follow the path down to another kissing gate.

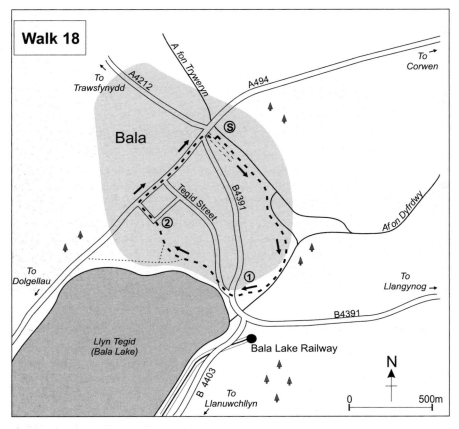

1. Follow the path along, past another weir and up to a road. To your left there is a bridge and just past this is the station for Bala Lake Railway. So if you approaching this walk by train you will need to cross the bridge and follow the directions from here.

   Go through the kissing gate, cross the road and turn right. Follow the road along the edge of the lake where there are lots of benches for you to stop and admire the view.

   There are fantastic views of the lake from this road.

   Turn left through a kissing gate just before you reach a car park. Follow the path until you come to a fork where you turn right

Weir on Afon Trweryn, Bala

down to a kissing gate. Follow this gravel path along as it heads back into Bala.

2. Continue along this path, ignoring a turning to the left, until you come to a road with a car park and toilets ahead. Turn left and follow the road up to the A494 through the centre of Bala. Turn right and walk along the pavement through the centre of town. You will pass several tea shops, pubs and a selection of other shops on route.

After you have walked through town you will come to the right turn down to the car park.

In the area:

Bala Lake Railway (Rheilffordd Llyn Tegid; www.bala-lake-railway.co.uk) runs from Llanuwchllyn to Bala and return trips take up to 1.5 hours. The train travels along the eastern shore of Lake Bala with fantastic views throughout the trip. There is a café at

Llanuwchllyn Station. Trains run between March and October and there are some Santa specials in December.

Lake Vyrnwy (www.stwater.co.uk) is a walkers' paradise with many footpaths and nature trails to explore. There is a Sculpture Park in the woodland below the dam which celebrates the diversity of wild-life. There are sculptures from both local and international artists all made from local timber and on site materials. The RSPB visitor centre has a shop and café and there are picnic sites around the lake.

Walk 19: Tomen-y-Mur and Sarn Helen, Trawsfynydd

Allow: *2 hours 30 minutes*

Tomen-y-Mur and Sarn Helen are a Roman military complex and road, set in beautiful scenery to the south of Trawsfynydd. Though all you can see now are earthworks in the field (partly obscured by vegetation in summer), the site is special due to the presence of ancillary buildings in addition to the military fort. These buildings included an amphitheatre, bath-house, *mansio* (guest-house), practice earthworks, leats, roads and burial monuments.

The walk takes you along stony tracks and through fields and the going is much rougher than it would have been in Roman times! This is definitely not a winter walk as the farm land is very muddy in wet weather.

Map: Ordnance Survey 1:25000 Explorer OL18 – grid reference 706388

Distance: 3½ miles (5.5km)

Getting there: Take the small road just south of the Betws-y-Coed turning off the A487/A470. Head under a railway bridge and park in the car park on the right just before the cattle grid.

Turn right out of the parking area, cross over the cattle grid (or through the gate on the right) and walk up the road. When you reach the first bend in the road turn down the track on the right that is marked as a footpath.

> There are great views on the right. The small mound is a medieval castle motte, Tomen-y-Mur (11th century), which was built over the ramparts of the Roman fort. Beyond this you can see Llyn Trawsfynydd, a large lake and reservoir. This was dammed to provide power for the Trawsfynydd nuclear power station (now decommissioned). The scenery around the lake was also used in the

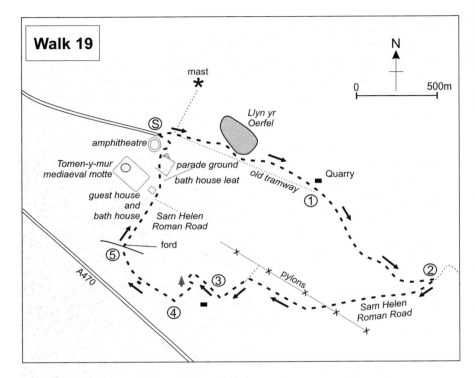

filming of "First Knight". Across the lake are the two Rhinogs, separated by a deep pass.

This gravel track leads you all the way to a slate quarry. On the way you will pass a small lake (Llyn yr Oerfel) on the left. You will then see a long line of slate on the right which is the remains of the quarry tramway.

Although most of the slate quarry is in ruins there is still some slate cutting going on at this site.

1. Walk past the quarry and continue down the track ahead. The track begins to get rougher and at times it is easier to walk alongside it.

As you walk along the track you will see fantastic views over the Llafar and Prysor valleys ahead.

2. The track eventually brings you down to a junction in the path with a sheep pen on the right and a small waterfall ahead. Turn right here walking on the lower path almost back in the direction you came. Stay on this track, ignoring the small path off to the right, with the stone wall just below you on the left.

This track follows the Roman road, Sarn Helen.

This section of the track can be quite tough going and winds its way round reeds. It leads you up to a gate-

Route finding!

way and into a grass field. At the far corner of this field you will see two gates. Go through the gate on the left and follow the track along the left-hand edge of the field towards the farm.

3. Just before the farm turn right along the permissive path which goes in the direction of the Castle motte (Tomen-y-Mur). Follow this track through the gate ahead in the direction of the footpath arrows.

When you reach the wall at the far end of the field turn left over the ladder stile. You will have to lift the pushchair over the fence at the side of the stile. Cross the bridge over the stream and turn right down the grass field.

4. Go through the gate at the end of the field and down the small slope onto the track below. Turn right and go through the gateway ahead following signs to the amphitheatre. Follow this grassy track, ignoring any tracks to the side.

   Go through another gateway and follow the track ahead. The track will then bend round to the right and through another gate. After this do not go through the next gate ahead but turn right staying within the same field and follow the stone wall on your left. Tomen-y-Mur is on your left.

5. Go through the gateway at the far left corner of the field. Cross the ford over the stream and go up the hill to the gateway ahead. Be careful here, this section of the track can be very slippery.

   Follow the path through the gateway and up to the top of the field.

   All the lumps and bumps in the field ahead mark the spots of various features of the Roman fort (outlined on the map), including a bath-house, mansio (guest house), parade ground and water leats.

   Go through the gateway and turn right along the path.

   On your left are the remains of the Roman amphitheatre, which is thought to have been used for weapon training.

   This path brings you back to the road where the walk began. Turn left, cross the cattle grid and find your car.

In the area:

TrawsAqua: a new and exciting outdoor centre, open all year, on the edge of Llyn Trawsfynydd with canoe, mountain bike and rowing boat hire for all the family. For the less energetic there are trips around the lake on the lake launch, a café and picnic area.

Coed-y-Brenin Forest Park, south of Trawsfynydd, offers biking and walking trails. The visitor centre has a café and adventure playground.

Walk 20: Morfa Dyffryn, Harlech

Allow: *1 hour 30 minutes*

If you fancy a change from the mountains then this is the walk for you. This is a fantastic beach walk which has spectacular coastal views and takes you past some stunning sand dunes that are now a site of special scientific interest. The ridges of this extensive dune system enclose many wet hollows and small dunes which support a range of summer flowering plants and some rare birds including the ringed plover which is very vulnerable as it nests in bare sand.

Why not bring a picnic and some swimming kit and make a day of it?

Map: Ordnance Survey 1:25000 Explorer OL18 – grid reference 572227

Distance: 3 miles (5km)

Getting there: When driving north along the A496 from Barmouth, turn left down towards the beach and the Dyffryn Seaside Estate. Park in the beach car park at the end of this road. There are picnic tables and toilets here.

Walk to the far end of the car park and turn left up towards the beach. Walk up the boardwalk which takes you through the sand dunes and you will soon see the sea. Follow the boardwalk right along to the beach.

There is a picnic table on the way with a great view across the sea to the Lleyn Peninsula.

1. Turn right along the beach so you are walking along with the sea on your left. This walk can be lengthened or shortened to suit.

Morfa Dyffryn Nature Reserve is a Site of Special Scientific Interest due to its well preserved dune habitats. It lies at the junction of two marine sediment transport systems, leading to an extensive (7km long) and well-developed sand dune system. Dune

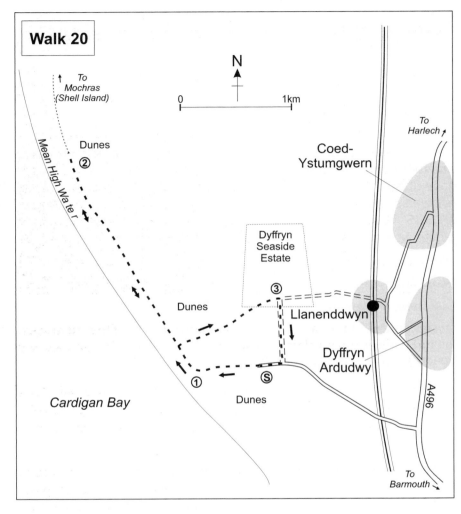

plants include hound's-tongue and sand cat's-tail as well as lyme and couch grasses. Interdune vegetation is also extensive in this area and can be seen from paths up into the dunes. These areas are colourful in the summer with plants including sharp sea-rush, marsh helleborine, orchids and the rare bog pimpernel. N.B. Do not climb the dunes or enter the interdune areas.

2. We suggest that you walk along the beach until you see the white

Morfa Dyffryn beach

sign warning you about the nude bathing zone. Then turn back and walk along until you see a fenced turning on the left with the red lifebuoy box number B34.

This is a very long beach and you can walk all the way to Shell Island (Mochras) when the tides are right. However, if you want to do this it does mean that you have to walk through an area of the beach which permits nude bathing!

Walk up the path over the dunes, onto the boardwalk and then through the gateway ahead. Follow the track to the caravan park. You will pass a playground, café and general stores on your right.

3. Take the second road on your right within the caravan park. There is a small roundabout at this junction and it is signposted as a bridleway. This road takes you out of the caravan park and at the end of this road, turn right, past the toilets to the car park.

In the area:

Shell Island (www.shellisland.co.uk) is a great place for kids as it has great sandy beaches and plenty of rock pools. The island can be reached by a tidal causeway and has great panoramic views on a fine day. There are large numbers of wild birds on the island and the estuary is a haven for all kinds of wildlife. The leisure complex has a snack bar, restaurant and a supermarket. There is also a gift shop and a camp shop.

Llanfair Slate Caverns and Children's Farm Park (www.lokalink.co.uk/harlech/slatecaverns). This is an old but important slate mine made over 100 years ago. Wander through the tunnels and chambers and then when you emerge from the caverns you get great views over Cardigan Bay. In addition there is a children's farm park here where the kids can cuddle baby rabbits and bottle-feed lambs and goats. There is also a nature and a woodland walk.

Walk 21: Eden Falls, Coed-y-Brenin, Dolgellau

Allow: 45 minutes

This walk is one of the forest trails in Coed-y-Brenin, a beautiful forest park north of Dolgellau. Coed-y-Brenin area is renowned for its mountain bike trails and woodland scenery, but also boasts some interesting and beautiful woodland trails.

The walk starts at the café and takes you along the banks of the Afon Eden along woodland paths, rocky in places, to a small waterfall, the Eden Falls. Leaflets on a woodland nature trail along this route are available for older children to spot the animals and answer a quiz.

Map: Ordnance Survey 1:25000 Explorer OL18 – grid reference 714278

Distance: 1 mile (2km)

Getting there: Park at the Coed-y-Brenin visitor centre, located off the A470 between Trawsfynydd and Dolgellau, north of Ganllwyd. There is a fee for parking.

From the car park, look for the white footprint sign marking the start of the forest trails. The start of the walk is marked by a red waymarker signposted "Afon Eden". Head down the small, bumpy forest path to turn left along the banks of the River Eden.

Pick your way to find the easiest route through the rocks and tree roots.

> There are picnic tables at intervals along this section of the route which is through broad-leaved woodland. Note the abundant mosses on boulders and tree trunks.

Go through the gap in a dry stone wall and continue along the path, now through Douglas firs. This section is bumpy with tree roots.

Walk 21

Afon Serw

③

slab ⟩⟩

wall

Afon Eden

④

①

②

S

N

Shop   WC

Café

0   500m

1. Go up hill through a rocky patch and carry on towards a wooden
bench. At the top of the hill turn right over a small footbridge and
carry on through the woods along a gravel path.

Go down 11 easy steps to a bridge and picnic table by the river. Go
over the narrow bridge and up 9 steeper steps on the far side.

Once over the bridge, go through the trees. The path here is very
rocky, but most of the rocks can be avoided by weaving through
the tree trunks nearer the river.

2. Follow the red waymarkers round to the left.

There are abundant boulders thick with moss in this part of the forest.

Negotiate the tree roots and go over a third footbridge. Go over four easy steps on the far side of the footbridge and follow the red waymarkers. The path improves about 20m after this bridge.

Meander through tall Douglas firs. Look out for the animals on posts, which form part

Walking amongst Douglas firs

of the nature trail in the forest. You will come to a badger first.

3. Carry on along the path, ignoring small paths to the left and right until you see a broad track. Do not go onto this track but follow the path to the right.

Follow the path as it bends round to the left, past a rocky slab and at the next junction turn left following the red sign.

4. Head down the track for about 30m and take the path off to the right, marked by a red footprint. Go past a fox and follow the path down the hill.

Where the path joins a gravel track, turn right and walk along the track back to the car park.

In the area:

Bro Ddyfi Leisure Centre, Machynlleth offers a variety of activities including a swimming pool, with flume and fun sessions, climbing wall, gym, health suite and coffee shop. There is even a crèche on certain weekdays, but you will need to book this in advance (http://broddyfileisure.powys.gov.uk) .

Harlech Castle (01766 780552) is spectacularly situated on a rocky outcrop high above the sea. It was one of Edward I's "iron ring" of castles across Wales, designed to contain the Welsh, and is now a world heritage site. There is plenty of open space and there are toilets and a gift shop on site.

Walk 22: Waterfalls and Goldmines, Coed-y-Brenin, Dolgellau

Allow: *2 hours 30 minutes*

The famous and rare Welsh Gold, used in royal wedding rings, has been mined in the Dolgellau gold belt since the 1840s. There are old mine workings along this route, so keep children (large and small!) under control.

This walk takes you up easy forestry tracks in a beautiful wooded valley, now part of the Coed-y-Brenin forest, to the Mawddach and Pistyll Cain waterfalls. You can also see the remains of Gwynfynnydd goldmine, which was operational from the 1860s. Extraction from earlier waste is still continuing today, though mining stopped in 1999.

Map: Ordnance Survey 1:25000 Explorer OL18 – grid reference 733261

Distance: 2½ miles (4km)

Getting there: Turn off the A483 down a small no through road at the speed limit sign north of Ganllwyd. Carry on down the road, ignoring a left turn to a house. Continue through the forest and park at the Tyddyn Gwladys car park (picnic tables).

From the car park turn right along the road, following the yellow marker posts – the start of the trail is signposted at the car park entrance, but we are doing a shorter version of the walk!

The tarmac ends after about 50m, and you carry on along a broad gravel track. Go through the gate marked "Ferndale".

Ferndale, now holiday accommodation, was originally the stables, offices and workshops of a blasting powder works connected with mining in the valley.

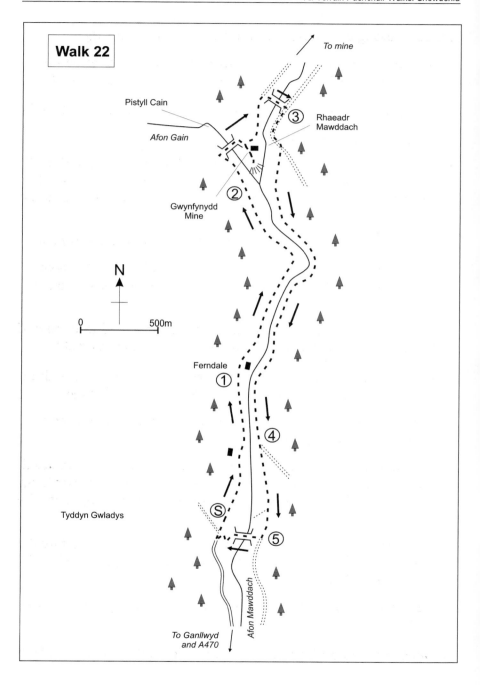

Continue along the track, with the river down to your right.

> You can see the remains of mine workings in the woods along this route, the first of which are buildings and inclines up to your left.

1. Go behind "Ferndale" and through the barrier up the gravel track.

> There is a flooded mine adit just before the barrier.

Continue on the level track, ignoring a private road up to the left. The track carries on the level and bends round to the left. Don't go down the mountain bike track which heads steeply down to the river.

The track is rocky for a short distance and then starts to rise.

> The white pebbles along the track are quartz, which was the host mineral for the gold. The gold occurs as the native metal in quartz veins in the rock.

Continue past more abandoned mine workings and into view of the Rhaeadr Mawddach waterfall in the river to your right.

2. The track heads up the left tributary, which flows through an impressive, small, rocky gorge. Go onto the metal bridge.

> From the bridge you can see Pistyll Cain waterfall; a narrow spout cascading into the rocky gorge.

Continue along the track to Gwynfynydd Mine – now disused. Turn right, downhill, to a viewpoint in front of the mine workings overlooking the two rivers. Take care as the steep drops into the river are not protected.

Retrace your steps back up to the main track and turn right up the hill. Follow the river and head round to the right crossing the river by the stone bridge.

> The track straight ahead is a public footpath leading to the working goldmine.

3. Once over the bridge follow the track down the opposite side of the river. Head up to a T-junction and turn right, ignoring the mbm mountain bike trail arrow.

The track surface improves as you go down the valley and opposite "Ferndale" it starts to rise again.

4. At the next junction, take the right-hand fork down hill.

There are abundant mosses and ferns in the forest, an indication of suitable damp conditions along the river banks.

Rocky gorge on the Afon Mawddach

Opposite the car park, continue on the main track. Ignoring a track to the right which leads to stepping stones that are unsuitable for pushchairs.

5. At the next junction, marked by both blue and yellow posts, take the right-hand fork down to a footbridge.

This bridge was new at time of writing and was not shown on either the forestry leaflet or the OS map.

Cross over the bridge, pausing to look at the rocky canyon of the Afon Mawddach. On the other side, head up a short but steep forest path to the road. Turn right on the road and head back to the car park.

In the area:

Machinations in Llanbrynmair (www.machinations.org.uk) is Britain's only exhibition of automata (moving figures) which will captivate the whole family. There is a café and children's play area, and the shop sells "Timberkits" moving models to build at home.

Greenstiles Cycle Hire (www.greenstiles.com) offers bike hire for all the family. Shops are located in Dolgellau and Machynlleth and as well as a fleet of bikes they have a number of child seats, buggies and trailers.

Walk 23: Panorama Walk, Barmouth

Allow: *45 minutes*

Panorama Walk is one of the most popular walks in this area. The walk is only short but takes you to a spectacular viewpoint where you can see the whole length of the Mawddach estuary with the Cadair mountain range to the south and Diphwys to the North.

The route takes you along both grass and woodland paths and can be a little rocky in places. However, the viewpoint is well worth the effort and there is a bench allowing you to stop for a while and admire the view.

Map: Ordnance Survey 1:25000 Explorer OL23 – grid reference 625165

Distance: 1 mile (1.6km)

Getting there: Drive along the A496 to Barmouth and turn right up the no-through road, if you pass the entrance to the footbridge on your left you have just gone too far. Follow the road up round some houses and go right at the fork in the road. Eventually you will see a signpost for the Panorama Walk and immediately after this a car park.

Walk back down the road and turn left down the gated track signposted to Panorama Walk. Follow this grassy path along for about five minutes until you come to a gateway.

1. Go through this gate and then turn immediately right through a second gate. Follow this stony track as it heads into woodland. You will come to a fork in the track where you turn right. Don't go left up the steps.

2. After fifteen minutes you will come to a fantastic view point and there is a bench here.

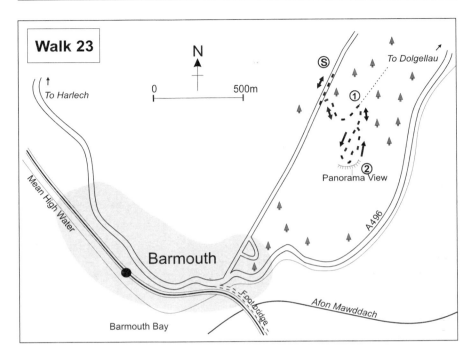

You will be able to see views across the whole estuary. To your right are Barmouth and the wooden bridge over the estuary. Straight ahead is the Cadair Idris mountain range on the other side of the estuary.

To return to your car you can either follow the path that you came along or you can continue on the path ahead which takes you down a series of stone steps. If you go down the stepped route turn right when you come to the junction.

Follow the path back to the gate turn left and immediately go through the second gate. Return along this grassy path which takes you back to the road. Turn right, walk up the road and find your car.

In the area:

Barmouth Beach has miles of unbroken golden sand as well as safe paddling and bathing waters. There are traditional donkey rides,

Barmouth Bridge and Fairbourne Spit

swing boats and amusement arcades providing amusement for all
the family.

Barmouth Pavillion Leisure Centre (01341 280111) has both a
swimming pool and an indoor climbing wall providing entertain-
ment if the weather isn't so good.

Walk 24: Morfa Mawddach, Barmouth.

Allow: *2 hours 30 minutes*

The Mawddach Trail is a nine mile route which runs the length of the Mawddach Estuary from Dolgellau to Barmouth. The trail follows the path of a dismantled railway and, therefore, the track is flat and very easy going all the way. Our route follows just a small section of the trail from Arthog to Barmouth and then returns on footpaths along the estuary edge. The route crosses the Mawddach Estuary at the half mile long Barmouth Bridge which was built in 1867. The bridge carries both trains and pedestrians and gives magnificent views of both the coastline and the estuary.

There are plenty of variations to do on this walk. You could catch the train back from Barmouth to Morfa Mawddach Station, or catch the ferry to Fairbourne and walk back from there. The Mawddach Trail also runs all the way to Dolgellau so you could start the walk at any point you wish.

Map: Ordnance Survey 1:25000 Explorer OL23 – grid reference 640147

Distance: 4¾ miles (7.5km)

Getting there: Drive along the A493 and turn down the track along side a green corrugated tin hut signposted to Min-y-Don. You will immediately pass through a gateway and follow the road down until you see a small car park on the left. There is a picnic bench in the car park.

This car park is at the site of the old Arthog Railway Station on the Dolgellau-Barmouth railway. Leave the car park by the small wooden gate and walk up onto the old railway track. Turn left along this gravel track in the direction of the RSPB reserve.

1. Follow this track all the way to the next car park at Morfa Mawddach Station. You will pass Arthog Bog on your right and

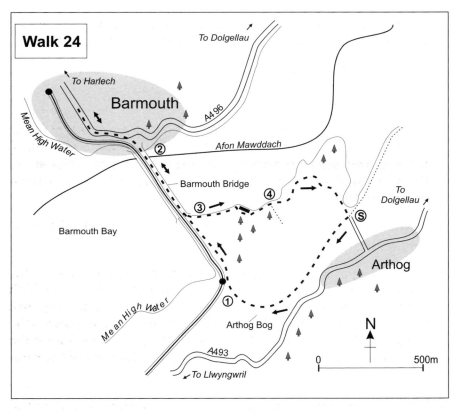

pass through a kissing gate and over a tarmac road on your way. There are picnic tables and toilets at this car park.

Arthog Bog is a small raised bog and a Site of Special Scientific Interest. It is home to many rare plants, birds and butterflies. Look out for reed bunting, mallard and curlew.

The track takes you alongside the railway track and you simply follow the path as it takes you over the Barmouth viaduct. There is a small toll (60p at the time of writing) to cross this bridge.

There are fantastic views over the sand dunes, estuary and surrounding hills from the bridge.

2. After the toll booth, walk up the track to the road. Cross over the road and turn left, following the pavement into Barmouth.

   There are plenty of tea shops, pubs and ice cream parlours in Barmouth. If you don't want to go into Barmouth you can simply turn back before you reach the toll booth.

   When you are done in Barmouth, return along the road towards the footbridge. Cross the road, go down the path to the footbridge toll and walk across the bridge. Go through the gate at the end of the bridge and go left over the stile. You will need to lift the pushchair over this.

   If you don't want to lift over this stile simply follow the trail back to the car park.

3. Walk straight across the grass and sand to the track round the small hill ahead. Some of this area is tidal so walk along which ever route you can. Follow the track as it follows the estuary edge until you see a terrace of houses ahead. Turn right just before the houses and follow the track around the back. Turn left after the houses and follow the track back alongside the edge of the estuary.

4. Turn right through a small gate just before the gateway ahead marked Bryn Celyn. Turn immediately left through another gateway and follow the footpath. Follow the path around to the right and then bear right down the footpath (Llwybr Cyhoeddus).

   Follow this grass track through the bracken and then through a small gateway on the right. Once you reach a road, turn right and follow the road back to the car park.

In the area:

Fairbourne and Barmouth Steam Railway has regular trains and even has many special events for children. You can learn about the railway history at the museum and see the wildlife at the Rowen Nature Centre at the station. There is also a shop and a café at the

On the Mawddach Trail

station. See the website for special events and opening times (www.fairbournerailway.com).

The Mawddach Trail is also a great cycle route and bikes can be hired at Birmingham Garage, Barmouth (01341 280644) and Greenstiles in Dolgellau (01341 423332).

Walk 25: Llys Bradwen, Cadair Idris

Allow: 1 hour

This is a nice easy walk that utilises permitted paths along farm tracks. There are fantastic views of Barmouth and the Mawddach estuary along the way as well as historical monuments to wander round.

Llys Bradwen (Court of Bradwen) lies alongside the River Arthog and now consists of two conjoined square enclosures cut into the hillside. This is thought to be a mediaeval site and most likely the court of a minor chieftain. Roman pottery has also been found at this site, suggesting it has a very long history.

If you want a nice spot for a picnic then drive back to the National Trust Cregennen Lakes where there are plenty of lovely places to sit and admire the views.

Map: Ordnance Survey 1:25000 Explorer OL23 – grid reference 656134

Distance: 1½ miles (2.5km)

Getting there: Drive along the A493 and take the turning signposted to Llynnau Gregennen (Cregennen Lakes) at Arthog. Follow this road up passing through two gateways. Pass the National Trust car park next to the lakes and continue up the road, through two more gates then turn right at the T-junction. Drive along this road (Ffordd Ddu) and park on the verge after the next gate.

Walk back through the gateway and, shortly after, go through the wooden gateway on your left. This uneven grass path cuts across the field to another gateway and there are great views all round. Cross over a stony stream bed and then pass an area of woodland on your left.

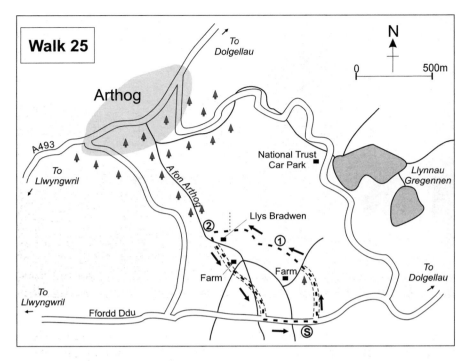

1. Go straight ahead through the gateway signposted Llwybr Cyhoeddus. This takes you between two walls. Follow the left-hand wall down and then turn right at the corner before the next wall (there are some arrows marked on the wall). Follow the track along this flat grass path to another gateway and follow the path straight ahead.

You will soon see great views out over the Mawddach estuary and the Barmouth railway bridge.

Go through the next gateway and keep following the track straight ahead. You will now be on a stony path which takes you through yet another gateway. Continue through the next gateway, don't take the track to your right.

2. As you go up this track you will see a river (Afon Arthog) to your right and a clapper bridge across it. If you want to avoid going through the ford, cross the river here.

Llyn Gregennen

On your left are the ruins of Llys Bradwen and if you look carefully you can make out the walls. The crag that you can see up ahead is Tyrrau Mawr.

If you follow this track up, it crosses the river at a ford. Go through the next gateway and follow the track found the farmhouse. Continue through another gateway and past a derelict building on your right.

Continue along this track passing through another gateway and to the road. There are great panoramic views as you go along this track. Turn left on to the road and walk down to your car.

In the area:

King Arthur's Labyrinth (www.kingarthurslabyrinth.co.uk). This is a boat trip along a subterranean river with a great waterfall and a labyrinth of tunnels and caverns. The tales and legends of King Arthur are told along the route. Open from March to November. Also on this site is Corris Craft Centre where there is a small selection of craft shops selling wooden toys and many other goods. There is also an adventure playground and a restaurant.

Celtica (www.celticawales.com) takes you back in time to discover the history and culture of the Celts. There is an audiovisual show, exhibitions and reconstructions to see. There is plenty for the kids to do with an indoor soft play area, face painting, workshops, activities and dressing up. There are also tearooms, a shop and extensive grounds to wander around.

Walk 26: Ffordd Ddu, Cadair Idris

Allow: *2 hours 30 minutes*

Ffordd Ddu (Black Road) is an ancient road over the shoulder of Cadair Idris, from Dolgellau to Llanegryn. It is renowned for its extensive archaeological remains and runs across rugged moorland with spectacular views over the Mawddach estuary.

The walk is mainly along stony tracks and metalled road, but the middle section heads down across farmland which is boggy in places and there are a couple of fords, so make sure your boots are waterproof!

Map: Ordnance Survey 1:25000 Explorer OL23 – grid reference 648134

Distance: 3 miles (5km)

Getting there: Drive from the A493 up the small turning signposted Llynau Gregennen (Cregennen Lakes). Follow the narrow gated road to the lakes (toilets and information in the lake car park). Carry on past the car park to a T-junction. Turn right and go through four more gates. Park before the fifth gate, which is at a signposted turning down to a farm (Cregennen).

From the road turn left at the gate marked "Cregennen Farm" to follow a grassy track up hill, steep at times, to a gate.

As you look back you get a good view of the crags above Llynau Gregennen, and you can see a standing stone on a rise just to the right of a small plantation.

1. Go through the gate and turn right onto the rough tarmac road, Ffordd Ddu (Black Road).

Straight ahead is another standing stone on the ridge in front of the skyline.

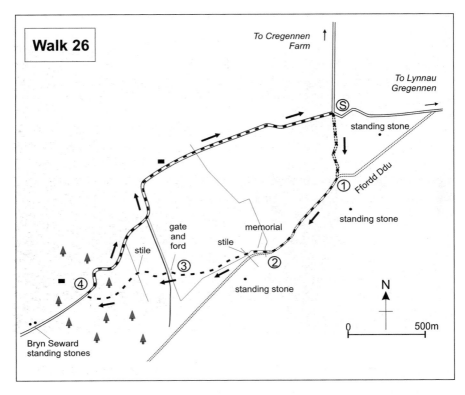

Continue up the road, which is now stony, and through a gate.

Behind you, you can just see Llynnau Gregennen.

Carry on along the track, with a view over the sea to the Lleyn Peninsula and Bardsey Island, Barmouth and the Fairbourne Spit. On a very clear day you may be able to see the Wicklow Mountains in Ireland.

2. Just before the track begins to level off, turn right to follow a wall, marked by a Public Footpath sign. The going gets rougher here and the ground is locally boggy.

Cross a small stream, and follow the wall to a stile.

The wall bears a plaque in memory to the 20 airmen of the 351st Bombardment Group of the USAAF, killed in the crash of a B17G

Ffordd Ddu

Flying Fortress on this hillside June 8th, 1945, with a list of their names.

Lift over the stile and go into the next field, following the grassy path through reeds heading towards the plantation.

The ground is wet in places, and this walk is likely to be very wet in winter, but there are wonderful views of the Mawddach Estuary.

3. At the end of the field, go through the gate next to a ladder stile (this gate was loose, so open with care!), cross another small stream and continue on the track. Once through the gate, the ground is drier and the view continues to open out to your right.

Head down the field, to a bank of stones heading to a sheep fence. Lift the pushchair over the small stile and continue along the track into the plantation. The track is muddy in the plantation as it is used by mountain bikes.

Follow the track down to the road and turn right.

For an archaeological detour, turn left at the road. After about half a mile at the end of the plantation are two standing stones, the Bryn Seward stones.

4. Walk along the road as it winds along the hillside past isolated farms and there are numerous gates to open! Follow the road back to your car.

In the area:

The **Centre for Alternative Technology** near Machynlleth (www.cat.org.uk) was set up to find solutions to the world's environmental problems. Set in 7 acres in an old quarry, there are interactive displays, organic gardens and the café specialises in vegetarian and fair trade food. There is an eco-adventure playground and a "mole-hole". Access is via a water-balanced railway and all toilets are composting!

Abergwynant Farm Pony Trekking near Dolgellau (www.abergwynantfarm.com) has an extensive range of horses and ponies suitable for all ages and abilities. Helmets are provided. Treks are usually 2 hours long, and paddock rides are available for children.

Walk 27: Tan-y-Coed Falls, Corris

Allow: 1 hour

Tan-y-Coed woodland is a mixed woodland of native broad-leafed species and coniferous plantation. In the valley bottom a picturesque river tumbles down a rocky chasm in a narrow waterfall.

The walk is through pleasant woodland along forestry tracks and small paths. There is a very narrow rocky cleft to negotiate, which results in the advanced "wheelbarrow" pushing technique! But the view of the falls is well worth it.

Map: Ordnance Survey 1:25000 Explorer OL23 – grid reference 755054

Distance: 1 mile (2km)

Getting there: Park in the Forestry Commission car park south of Corris on the A487 (fee). There are toilets in the car park (but no changing facilities) and lots of picnic tables.

From the car park, walk back down the road to the Forestry Commission sign and head along the wide track straight ahead. Walk up the track through pleasant oak and beech woodland, ignoring minor paths to the right.

1. Ignore the left path marked with yellow posts and continue up the track to a cross-roads just past a lay-by. Turn left here, following the red and green footprint signs.

   This part of the walk is part of the woodland nature trail (unsuitable for pushchairs); leaflets are available outside the toilet block in the car park.

   Follow the grassy track. There are tree roots to negotiate at the start of the path, but these decrease after about 10 metres. Follow the path round to the left at the butterfly and zigzag downhill heading towards the sound of the waterfall.

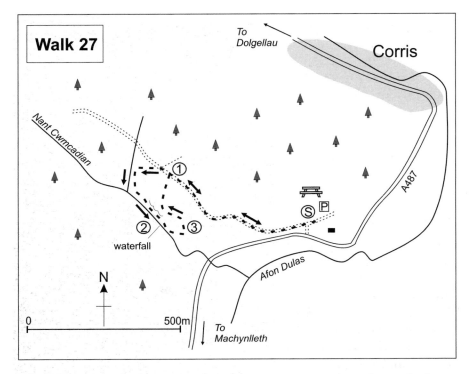

The path levels out to follow the river bank. Follow the path along the river until you come to a narrow rock cleft.

This is passable but requires some advanced ATP technique! Remove the back wheels of the pushchair and "wheelbarrow" the pushchair through the rock cleft. On the far side (about 5m) replace the wheels.

2. Through the chasm is a fantastic view of the waterfall as it cascades down a rocky canyon.

Continue along the path, now level, through woodland consisting of birch, beech and oak.

Note the abundant ferns and mosses which thrive in the damp conditions by the stream.

3. Follow the path, now stony, round to the left and back uphill. Just

past the mole is a steep section with roots – pull or lift over these. Continue up the hill and pull over a last very steep lip to regain the forestry track.

Turn right and follow the track back to the car park.

In the area:

Corris Railway and Museum: The Corris Railway was the first narrow gauge railway in Mid-Wales, built in 1859. You can take a trip on the restored railway in one of the steam trains, and visit the museum, which has extra exhibitions in the

The wheelbarrow technique!

summer months (www.corris.co.uk)

Woodland Nature Trail is unfortunately not suitable for pushchairs, but small children will enjoy answering the quiz questions and looking for the animal markers along the way. Follow the red footprints from the car park – leaflets are available from tourist information centres and outside the toilet block in the car park.

Walk 28: Nant Gwernol, Abergynolwyn

Allow: *1 hour 30 minutes*

This quiet valley used to be the site of the Bryn Eglwys Slate Quarry which was started in 1844 by John Pugh of Penegoes. The quarry was extended twenty years later employing over 300 men, houses were built in Abergynolwyn and the Talyllyn Railway constructed. The quarry finally closed in 1946 and the land was acquired by the Forestry Commission and the Woodland Trust.

This walk takes you through the woodland of Coed Nant Gwernol and past Nant Gwernol Station, which is situated in a natural ravine. There are remnants of the Bryn Eglwys Slate Quarry to see on route. The walk heads downstream past mountain waterfalls and back down to Abergynolwyn. On the whole the paths are excellent but there is one section above Nant Gwernol Station that may require two people.

Map: Ordnance Survey 1:25000 Explorer OL23 – grid reference 677069

Distance: 2¾ miles (4.5km)

Getting there: Park in Abergynolwyn car park opposite the Railway Inn.

From the car park, turn left onto the main road and walk along the pavement. Pass a children's playground on your right.

1. Turn left past a cottage with a sign to the station on it. This takes you up the Abergynolwyn forestry commission track which is also marked as a footpath. Follow this broad woodland track as it turns to the right.

   Cross over the railway track and continue up hill. As you walk up the track you will come to a large clearing. Turn left following the red markers in the direction of Nant Gwernol Station.

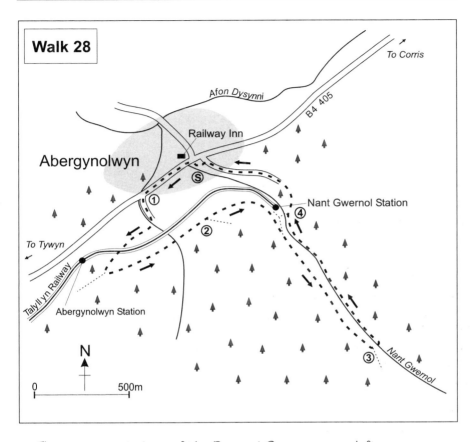

There are great views of the Dysynni Gorge on your left.

2. When you come to a fork in the path continue straight ahead following the red markers. Continue following this broad wood-land track and you will come to a clearing with great views of Cadair Idris ahead. The path then bends round to the right and heads into the woodland.

You will come to a fork in the path, take the right-hand path marked with a yellow and purple marker. Don't go down the steep downhill path. Be careful of the steep slope on your left.

When you get to the top of this track, passing over a few awkward rocks on the way, you will have to cross some old railway lines. Go past the information board and follow the track ahead.

The track then opens out and there is a fantastic view of the valley to the left. Look out for waterfalls in the river below. There is also a bench along this route, which makes a nice picnic spot.

The Tal-y-Llyn Railway

3. Shortly after the bench you will see a footbridge over the river. After this you will come to a junction. Take the left-hand path (awkward) down to the footbridge (yellow and blue markers). Go over the footbridge where you get great views both up and down stream.

After the footbridge turn left and follow the path downhill with the river on your left. Follow this beautiful riverside path as it heads slowly downhill down into the bottom of the valley.

4. When you come to a fork in the track take the right-hand path. Don't go down the steps to the footbridge. This track takes you up and away from the river. Follow the broad grassy track all the way to a gateway. The kissing gate is too narrow so you will have to lift the pushchair over the gate.

Turn left and walk down the road. This road brings you all the way back down to Abergynolwyn and at the end of the road you will find the car park. If you need refreshments the Railway Inn has great food and beer, lots of outdoor tables and toilets with baby changing facilities. There are also toilets and a café in the car park.

In the area:

Dysynni Cycle Route takes you round the calm and quiet Dysynni valley. The route passes the ruins of Castell y Bere (a 13th-century mountain fortress built by Llewelyn the Great) and the 760 foot high cliff Craig yr Aderyn (Bird Rock is thought to be the only inland nesting site of the cormorant in Europe). Bikes with child seats can be hired from Bird Rock Cycle Hire, Bryncrug (01654 711550).

CJ's Fun Factory (01654 712717) is a new two-level indoor play area for children between the ages of 1-9. A great place to expel some of your child's energy when it's raining!

Walk 29: Dolgoch Falls, Abergynolwyn

Allow: *30 minutes*

This is a very easy but beautiful riverside walk which takes you to a pretty waterfall and then past the Tal-y-Llyn Railway. This walk can also be reached by train, making it a great day out for the kids. The Tal-y-Llyn Railway was built in 1866 for the Bryn Eglwys slate quarry and for passenger service. Dolgoch Falls Station was opened in 1873. The quarry closed in 1948 and the railway closed in 1950. Thanks to the Tal-y-Llyn Railway Preservation Society, it reopened in 1951 and Dolgoch became a popular tourist attraction.

Dolgoch Falls is a set of three magnificent waterfalls and this walk visits the lowest of these. There are a wide variety of plants in this beautiful gorge with different species seen on the northern and southern slopes. It is possible to extend the walk further up river to some more waterfalls, however, this route isn't pushchair friendly so you will need a papoose to do this.

Map: Ordnance Survey 1:25000 Explorer OL23 – grid reference 649046

Distance: ¾ mile (1.5km)

Getting there: Park in the Dolgoch Falls and Tea Rooms car park on the B4405. If you arrive by train follow the directions below from Dolgoch Station (number 2).

Walk to the top right corner of the car park, through the gate and turn left along the lane towards the station and the falls. You will pass the hotel and tea rooms on your left.

> The tea rooms are open 10.30am-4.30pm and for bar meals between 12.00-2.30pm. They also sell ice cream.

Go through the gate and continue straight ahead with the stream

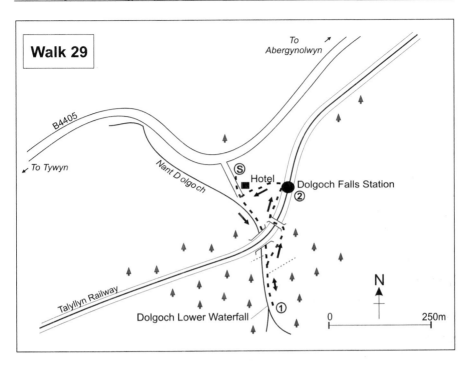

Walk 29

To Abergynolwyn

B4405

To Tywyn

Nant Dolgoch

Ⓢ ■ Hotel

● Dolgoch Falls Station ②

Talyllyn Railway

Dolgoch Lower Waterfall ①

N

0   250m

(Nant Dolgoch) on your right – don't turn left towards the station. A couple of minutes later you will pass under the railway viaduct. You will come to a footbridge on your right, don't cross this but continue straight ahead.

1. Eventually the path brings you up to a great view point for the lower waterfall. There are benches on the left here if you want to stop for a while and admire the view.

   Turn round and head back down the track for a minute or so and take the second turning on the right through some metal gates towards the station. This heads uphill for a short while and then bears left over a boarded walk to a gate. Cross the footbridge over the railway to a great picnic area.

2. Follow the path along to Dolgoch Falls Station and turn left immediately after the toilets following the way out sign. Follow the path down and through a gate. Turn left and go down the

track towards the tea rooms. There are a few steps on this track but as you are going downhill they are easy to push down.

Go through the gates, turn right, pass the tea rooms and find your car in the car park.

In the area:

Knightly's Fun Park (www.funfair-hire.com) has something for everyone. There is a family fun fair, a restaurant and a bingo hall! Well the kids will love it!

Tal-y-Llyn Railway runs from February to December but make sure you check the website (www.talyllyn.co.uk)

Lower Dolgoch Falls

for train times. The railway is the owner of the locomotive Douglas, which was written into the Rev. W. Awdry's stories as Duncan. This locomotive runs on several dates throughout the year. There is a railway museum at the Tywyn station as well as a café and shop.

Walk 30: Panorama Walk to Llyn Barfog, Aberdyfi

Allow: 1 hour

This is a lovely walk across open country with spectacular panoramic views over the Dyfi estuary and Borth Bog.

The route passes along farm tracks and takes you to the beauty spot at Llyn Barfog (Bearded Lake), so called because it is completely covered in aquatic plants. This lake, like many in Wales, is the setting for an Arthurian legend. A terrible monster, the *avanc*, is said to have lived in the lake and raided the surrounding countryside. When Arthur heard of this, he went to the lake and threw a chain around the *avanc*. Then, with the help of his horse, he pulled the creature from the lake and killed it.

Map: Ordnance Survey 1:25000 Explorer OL23 – grid reference 642980

Distance: 2 miles (3.5km)

Getting there: From Averdovey, go up Copperhill Road and turn right at the housing estate signposted to Bearded Lake. Turn left at the T-junction and continue up the hill. Take the right turn signposted Bearded Lake and go along this scenic hill-top road. Park in the lay by just before the second gate.

Go through the gate ahead and walk up the track towards Bwlch Farm. Then through the two gates next to the house and follow footpath sign up the stone and gravel track.

It will be immediately obvious why this is called panorama walk. There are spectacular views over the Dyfi estuary and Borth Bog to your right. Borth Bog is the largest raised bog in the country, famous for its variety of wetland plants and insects. Look for the gentle upward curve of the surface.

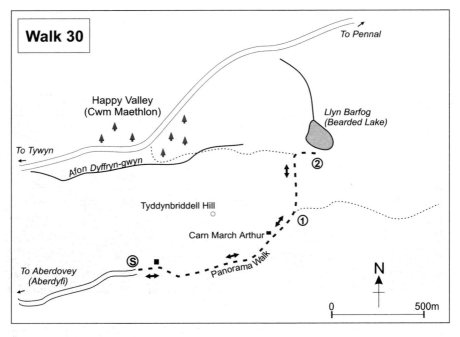

Keep following this track along as it turns to grass. Go through a gateway and follow the track along passing a stone on the left marked
Carn March Arthur, the Stone of Arthur's Horse.

> Look for a hoof-print etched into the rock here, which was
> supposedly made by Arthur's horse as it strained to pull the
> monster from the lake.

1. Go through the next gateway and you will see a fork in the path
   ahead of you. Take the left-hand track and follow this all the way
   to Llyn Barfog, ignoring a track off to the right. The lake is covered
   in water lilies in the summer.

> This area of Mid Wales provides one of the backdrops for "The Dark
> Is Rising" series of novels by Susan Cooper. In the last two books,
> "The Grey King" and "The Silver Tree", the author paints a literary
> portrait of the dramatic landscape, its myths and legends.
> Bearded Lake is the setting for one of the most magical scenes in
> the whole series!

Bearded Lake

2. If you fancy stopping for a while, there is a sheltered picnic spot on the path to the right.

Once you are ready to leave just follow the track back the way you came. So go through the first gateway, past the engraved stone and through four more gates. This takes you down past the farm and back to the lay by.

In the area:

Dyfi Discovery Cruises (www.dyfidiscoveries.co.uk) have boat trips around the mid-Wales coast. Cardigan Bay is home to Bottle-nose dolphins, porpoise, grey seals and many sea birds. Tales of local legends and heritage are told on route.

Halo Ice Cream Factory (www.haloshop.co.uk) has factory tours and the chance to meet the Honey Bear! Try the honey ice cream, watch the factory video and then browse the shop. Open every day March to October 10.00am-5.00pm.

Also from Sigma Leisure:

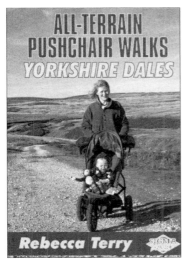

All-Terrain Pushchair Walks: Yorkshire Dales

Rebecca Terry

Find out the best of what the Yorkshire Dales has to offer with these 30 tried and tested all-terrain pushchair walks through open moorland and country estates, and alongside the beautiful and dramatic rivers for which this National Park is renowned. The walks are all accurately graded and have at-a-glance symbols making choosing easier. £7.95

All-Terrain Pushchair Walks: West Yorkshire

Rebecca Chippindale & Rebecca Terry

Pushchair-friendly routes in the spectacular countryside around the major towns of Keighley, Bradford, Leeds, Halifax, Huddersfield and Wakefield. There's woodland, moorland, canals, parks – and even some walks with a train journey in the middle – visiting a wide variety of locations including Ilkley Moor, Hardcastle Crags, Hebden Bridge and the River Wharfe. £7.95

All-Terrain Pushchair Walks: Peak District

Alison Southern

Level routes around Peak District villages and more adventurous (but safe) hikes across the moors. Alison is a parent of a young child and has an excellent knowledge of the Peak District. So now there's no reason to stay at home – here is the ideal opportunity to introduce the youngest children to the wide-open spaces of the Peak District! £7.95

All-Terrain Pushchair Walks: North Lakeland

Ruth & Richard Irons

Here are 30 walks across North Lakeland from Ennerdale Water to Lowther Park, Haweswater to Bassenthwaite. You'll find something to suit every type of walker – from Sunday Strollers to Peak Baggers and everyone else in between! Ruth and Richard Irons are experienced parents and qualified outdoor pursuits instructors – a reliable combination! £6.95

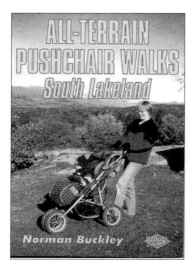

ALL-TERRAIN PUSHCHAIR WALKS: SOUTH LAKELAND
Norman Buckley
"This book is fantastic - a perfect guide for parents" - Kathleen Jones (Lakeland Book of The Year Awards, 2005). The companion volume to our popular 'All-Terrain Pushchair Walks for North Lakeland' published in the summer of 2003, this South Lakeland edition includes a collection of 30 walks specially-designed for the popular 'all-terrain' style of pushchair. Suitable for all the family - from tiny tots to grandparents - the pushchair friendly routes have a minimum of obstructions, are graded for ease of access and are accompanied by 'at-a-glance' descriptions. Enjoy fabulous Lakeland scenery - north to south, from Grasmere to Grizedale Forest, and west to east, from Coniston to Kendal - you'll be spoilt for choice! *£7.95*

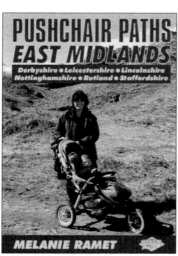

PUSHCHAIR PATHS: EAST MIDLANDS
Melanie Ramet
If you like walking but think you're restricted because of a child in a pushchair - this book proves you're not. This is the first pushchair-friendly walking book for the East Midlands written by enthusiastic walker, writer and 'East Midlander', Melanie Ramet.
Melanie has written 25 'ORPing' (Off-Road Pushchairing) routes - the term she feels best describes these routes. They have been written to allow unrestricted access into the heart of the wonderful East Midlands countryside, where walkers can be confident there will be no unexpected obstacles to negotiate the pushchair over, under or through! *£7.95*

All of our books are all available through booksellers. For a free catalogue, please contact: **SIGMA LEISURE, 5 ALTON ROAD, WILMSLOW, CHESHIRE SK9 5DY**

Tel/Fax: 01625-531035

E-mail: info@sigmapress.co.uk   Web site: www.sigmapress.co.uk